Guided Footsteps

Paula Gowdy

Copyright © 2015 by Paula Gowdy. All rights reserved.
Published in the United States by:
Soul Garden Press
P. O. Box 49
Malden-on-Hudson, New York 12453
Cover design: Turning Mill, Palenville, New York 12496

Gowdy, Paula
Guided Footsteps
ISBN: 978-0-9860936-1-6
1. Memoir   2. Inspirational Literature   3. Spirituality

DISCLAIMERS
Names and some characteristics of individuals portrayed in this book have been changed to completely protect the confidentiality of each.

Dedication

Guided Footsteps is dedicated to all those who are looking for the secrets that are hidden inside themselves.

* * *

"Each of us has a soul, but we forget to value it. We don't remember that we are creatures made in the image of God. We don't understand the great secrets hidden inside of us."

– Teresa of Ávila

Acknowledgments

Across six decades, countless people have entered my life and touched my heart. All of you have helped *Guided Footsteps* come to be. To each of you, I am grateful.

My deepest thanks go to my accomplished editor, Catharine Clarke. A kindred soul, Catharine turned the words I wrote into a book to share with others.

A heartfelt thank you goes to Reverend Dr. Lauren Artress, who introduced me to Catharine. Through her work with Veriditas, the organization that she founded, Lauren brings the healing power of the labyrinth to people from all walks of life, from all over the world.

To my lifelong friend, Chuck, I am forever grateful for your infinite patience, understanding, and trustworthiness. To my family and friends, your abiding love nourishes and enriches me. My heart goes out to all of you.

Every page of *Guided Footsteps* is an expression of my respect for the mystery of existence. Aware of an invisible thread that connects events in my life with Teresa of Ávila's life, I feel her presence as an inspiration that lives inside of me, allowing me to write this book.

Introduction

Throughout my life, secrets – a dark family secret and guarded inner secrets – have perpetually silenced my voice, kept me quiet about my childhood wounding and the deepest part of me, my connection to spirit.

Journaling, writing down how I feel, what I'm experiencing, has saved my life. It gives me back to myself, where my words allow me to speak, to hear and see the truth, my truth, offering me guidance from within.

In my late thirties and early forties, I witnessed a recurring, rectangular blue light that morphed into a dazzling golden, open book. This image inspired me to gather and organize my journal entries, including details of the mysterious events that had shaped my life, into a whole collection, a record I imagined sharing with others as a book. However, deep loss and consequent depressions halted me. Plagued with more questions than answers, I reached an impasse.

Twenty years later, nearing 60, I discovered the missing link, the key that tied past to present, learning about a spiritual woman from the sixteenth century, Teresa of Ávila, whose life experiences echo similar pivotal events in my own life. This allowed me to finish my story.

Through a series of vignettes, my story carries an essential message of abiding hope and unconditional love at the heart of every spiritual journey. I share my story that you, dear reader, may know you are not alone with your secrets. Your courage to share them, to tell your own story, may save your life.

My ongoing spiritual journey resonates with walking the labyrinth of life, a circuitous path to center and back, where forgivcness of oneself and others heals and makes whole, where every ending is a new beginning.

My Father and the Little Red Berry

In the backyard I see my father pick one little red berry from an evergreen bush. I wonder what he's doing. I walk over to him and ask him why he picked the berry off the bush. He says, "You'll see." He gently places the berry in a small pot of soil. Without saying a word, I follow my father into the house. I watch him turn on the kitchen faucet, put a little water in the pot and place it on the windowsill.

I look at the pot of soil every day, but it always looks the same. My father tells me to be patient and wait to see what happens. He shows me how to check the soil with my finger and how to water the plant if the soil feels dry. One day, after waiting for what seemed a long time, I see a tiny shoot pop out of the soil.

When the seedling is a few inches tall, my father carries the pot outside to the backyard. He picks a safe spot next to the foundation of the house. With his skillful hands, he carves a new home in the soil for the sprout and plants it in the ground. He gives the plant water and talks to it to help it grow.

My father takes great pleasure in raising and protecting this whisper of life. He watches the little red berry grow from a frail seedling into a sturdy bush.

* * *

After my father dies, I dig up the 23-year-old yew and plant it in my own yard. When I move from that home with my husband and our children, I'm sad to leave the now 30-year-old bush behind.

One day I'm back in town visiting with my sister-in-law, a breast cancer survivor. In the car, on our way back from lunch, we pass through my old neighborhood. When I spontaneously drive up the long driveway to my former home, we see a woman in the front pasture giving pony rides to a group of preschoolers.

My sister-in-law and I get out of the car and introduce ourselves to the new owner, who welcomes us into her home. My story about the sprawling bush near her front door touches her. The long-lived yew, much wider than it is tall, is now 50 years old.

My father died over 30 years ago, but his evergreen bush is still alive. He stimulated the potential inside the seed and initiated the new life. Love encouraged that bush to grow and thrive. All living things, in their uniqueness, are like bushes grounded in the earth. Each being carries within its nature a unique path to center, its true home.

The Kaleidoscope

A simple kaleidoscope is a cylinder with mirrors and small colored objects inside of it. When rotating this optical tube, the mirrors reflect the colorful objects as they tumble around inside. Light must enter the opposite end of the cylinder in order to see the movement of the brilliant colors and symmetrical patterns. Light awakens the beauty hidden inside a kaleidoscope.

* * *

I see my first kaleidoscope in the space that opens when I close my eyes. Bright colors and patterns freely move around in front of my closed eyes. I rub my eyes or squeeze them tighter to watch the colors and patterns change. When I close my eyes, I see the light.

My child's imaginary kaleidoscope is real. I find no difference between the world I see with my physical eyes and the world I experience inside. I naturally use my creative imagination to look inside myself.

* * *

The kaleidoscope is an ancient, reflective tool related to geometry. Specifically created angles reflect symmetrical, repetitive patterns. At the center of the kaleidoscope its geometric lines intersect much like a labyrinth.

Sacred geometry often (but not always) forms the basis of a labyrinth's pattern. Churches, temples, mosques and monuments are often built upon the foundation of sacred geometry. It is a value system in which the patterns, forms and mathematical proportions of the design relate to the order and nature of the universe.

The labyrinth is an ancient, sacred walking path widely used as a contemplative tool for spiritual reflection. The circuitous path leads from the threshold to the center of the labyrinth and from there returns back to the beginning. According to Reverend Dr. Lauren Artress, founder of Veriditas, the World-Wide Labyrinth Project, walking the labyrinth can "awaken us to the deep rhythm that unites us to ourselves and to the Light that calls from within."

* * *

When I am a senior in high school, I see the word "labyrinth" for the first time in my high school yearbook, *Echo*. The preface to the yearbook speaks to "sharing the never-ending path," the "labyrinth" of my high school life.

Getting Lost at the Beach

At a summer family reunion at the beach on the Connecticut shore, I overhear my older cousin say that he left his towel in the car. As everyone busily sets up beach chairs and umbrellas in the sand, I slip away to secretly retrieve my cousin's towel as a surprise for him. This cousin is special to me because he taught me a card trick that is still a mystery to me. I can't explain how or why it happens, but I'm thrilled every time the card trick works.

When no one is looking, I run barefoot through the sand to the parking lot. I walk up and down row after row in the sea of parked cars in search of my aunt's car. When a parking attendant sees me walking by myself, he asks me if I am lost. I tell him that I'm not lost, but I'm looking for the car to get my cousin's towel.

The man laughs, takes me by the hand and brings me to the parking booth. He picks me up and places me upon a tall wooden stool so I can see out the window. A second man in the booth tells me that I can have a lollipop.

* * *

I like my new friends and I really want that lollipop, but I am also anxious to find the car so I can get my cousin's towel and surprise him.

The second man opens the bag of lollipops. At the same time, I see my parents' car slowly driving toward the booth. As soon as I point out my mother and father to

Getting Lost at the Beach

the attendant, he plucks me off the stool and whisks me outside. He waves to my parents, and my father stops the car. When the man gently places me on my mother's lap, I notice that she is crying and wonder why.

Though happy to see my parents, in my four-year-old mind, all I can think about is that lollipop. Disappointed that my parents won't take me to my aunt's car so I can surprise my cousin with his towel, I try to explain to them that I wasn't lost when I walked in the winding rows through the parking lot.

The Helper

When my sister gets a new bicycle for her seventh birthday, I try to take the training wheels off my smaller bike but my parents stop me. They tell me that it's not safe. They say I'm too young to ride a two-wheeler. When they go inside the house, I walk my sister's bicycle down our short driveway into our quiet neighborhood street. For two hours I repeatedly climb up onto the seat and pedal as fast as I can.

That day, when I show my father how I learned to ride my sister's bicycle, he takes a wrench out of his toolbox and removes the training wheels from my bike.

* * *

That fall I'm too young to attend public school, so my parents enroll me in kindergarten at Saint Adalbert, the nearest parochial school. Sister Mary Amelda, my kindergarten teacher, lets me hide in the folds of the cloak she wears over her habit. I play with the wooden rosary beads that hang from her waist. I pass out paper and globs of gooey paste. I straighten tables and chairs. I press worksheets into a rectangular tray of jellied purple ink and crank the handle on the mimeograph machine to make copies. I walk to the rectory and to the convent to deliver messages to Father Paul and Mother Superior.

My kindergarten teacher tells my mother that I am the helper in school. She also tells my mother a secret: a helper doesn't need to be told what to do; a helper only needs to be asked to help. Now I'm the helper at home, too. My mother asks me to dust furniture, wash dishes, fold clothes, iron handkerchiefs and pillowcases and mop the floor. My father asks me to do yard work, clean the toolshed, remove nails from boards and paint the porch floor. I work hard to please my parents.

I play a game when I'm the helper. I look for jobs to do before my parents ask me for help. I race to finish these jobs in record time. I wait to see if my mother and father notice the surprise and I hope they tell me I've done a good job, that I'm a good girl.

Fear in First Grade

At my fortieth high school reunion, I chat with a man who had been one of my closest friends during our senior year. My heart smiles with memories of Riverside Park, trips to Dairy Queen, and the song, popular in the late 1960s, "Love is All Around." In high school this young man worked at a local variety store, and years later married the boss's daughter. A retired educator, he taught in our hometown at the same school where my dear friend, the woman who introduced me in high school to my future husband, is a special education teacher.

During our conversation I tell my old friend something that I've known all my life. Some 75 years ago, when my mother was confirmed in the Roman Catholic Church, she chose her best friend's name, Jean, as her confirmation name. Jean's daughter, one of my early childhood friends, is this man's wife.

At the reunion my husband and I sit at a table and talk with two men who were in kindergarten and first grade with me at St. Adalbert Parochial School. I confess to them that I don't know the name of the nun who was our first grade teacher. They say her name twice, but I still don't remember it.

* * *

In first grade, I sit at my desk to read about Dick, Jane and Spot. I write numbers on plain paper, and I write my name on lined paper. I learn how to say some words in

Fear in First Grade

Polish. When the teacher asks a question, I try to hide in my seat. I know what happens if I give a wrong answer.

The teacher steps out of the classroom. One first-grade girl is the room monitor. Her job is to tell the teacher the name of anyone who talks. Someone near me sneezes, so I quietly say, "God bless you." The room monitor reports me to the teacher for talking. The teacher puts me in the pitch-black stairway that leads from the basement of the church to the sacristy upstairs.

When it's time to start second grade, I refuse to go back to the parochial school. I hide under my parents' bed. My mother finds me, but she can't reach to pull me out from under the bed. She tries to coax me, and then she threatens me with "the belt," but I don't flinch. The next day my mother enrolls me in public school where second grade is already in session.

* * *

Thirty years later, my mother and I talk about my two years in parochial school. We talk about our visits with Sister Mary Amelda after she retired from teaching kindergarten. I tell my mother about my first-grade punishments. I tell her how I stood in the corner, got whacked on the knuckles with a ruler and spent time alone in the unlit stairway or in the dark coatroom. I tell her about the woman in the kitchen who put a bar of soap in my mouth. I even tell her about the steam rising from the pot of boiling water on the kitchen stove.

Fear in First Grade

* * *

The first-grade teacher brings me to the woman in the kitchen. The woman picks me up by my waist, holds out my arm and threatens to burn my hand in the hot steam. I kick and squirm and fight to free myself from her grip. I am so scared that I don't make a sound. Finally, so tired, I go limp, and the woman puts me down. I run away from her and hide in the coatroom.

* * *

My mother is astonished to learn about my first-grade punishments. Now she knows why I refused to go back to the parochial school when I was a little girl. I never told my mother about my first-grade fears because, even then, she never asked and I didn't have the words to tell her. At the end of this conversation my mother, a loving grandparent, says that she wishes she had been as good a mother to me as I am to my children.

I hold many experiences inside of me that I carry as secrets, even from myself, though they shape and define who I am. But I know I'm not alone on my life's path, as I search for truth and meaning.

The Old Dirt Path

My father's lifelong friend, a cousin, visits our house. He drives a Cadillac and wears a business suit. I sit on his lap when he talks to my parents. He takes us for a ride in his car to see several stores that he has recently opened. He tells my father and mother that they can own a store of their own.

My parents agree to invest in a coin-operated laundry business. My father's cousin offers to handle all the paperwork so my parents don't have to spend any money on a lawyer. At first my father says he isn't comfortable with this idea, but his cousin says, "Trust me."

My parents give me permission to tell one person about the new business. All day at school I think about what I will say to my friend. After school, about halfway along the same old dirt path that we walk home together every day, I tell her I have a secret. I share my secret with her and tell her that she is the only person, other than my family, who knows.

My friend is also a cousin. After school she teaches me to twirl a baton. She shows me how to work the strings on a marionette. When we go inside her house for a snack, her older brother and older sister speak to her and she whispers something back to them.

A few months after sharing my secret, I find out that the investment in the coin-operated laundry is a scam. My father's cousin is a master con artist. My parents' hard-earned money is gone.

* * *

It's easy to be fooled when someone you know and love says, "Trust me." Real trust comes from the heart, from a feeling deep inside that rings true.

* * *

When the circus comes to town, the three-ring tent, the trained animals and hundreds of circus-goers trample the path and stomp down the weeds that grow alongside of it. In time, after the circus leaves, the dirt path returns to its old shape. The Town Hall now sits on the site of the old dirt path. Underneath the structure and weight of the building, I know that the path is still there.

A Bargain

My father works in the family business, a neighborhood meat and grocery store. My aunt, her husband, and their four sons live in the big house over the store where my grandparents also lived when they were alive. After school I walk to the store to see if my father has a job for me to do. I take one look at my father and know that he is sick. I follow him up the stairs into my aunt's kitchen. He makes his way into the living room and passes out on the couch. He is still unconscious when the doctor arrives.

I go out the back door into the yard while the doctor examines my father. Straight ahead I gaze at the apartment house behind the store. When I was born, the apartment on the second floor was my first home. I look left and see the backs of the buildings that face the street around the corner from the store. An invisible line separates the backyards of these buildings from the side yard of the big house. I wander into the garden in that side yard and stare at the back door of the forbidden building where the gypsies live. Their colorful clothes fascinate me.

Vivid pictures form in my eleven-year-old mind: I see my grandmother's lifeless body on the couch in the living room where my father lays now. When an aunt forces me to kiss my grandmother good-bye, her face is cold on my lips.

One bitter-cold winter, my grandfather dies on the day after Christmas. For the first time, I see tears in my

A Bargain

father's eyes. He is sick with pneumonia when he goes to the funeral.

I see my baby cousin in her tiny casket. The second child in her family to die, she had a sister who died before she was born.

In my mind I hear my Nana's chair crash onto the kitchen floor. She is still seated in the overturned chair after she and the chair fall over backwards. The siren in the arriving ambulance pierces my ears. Two men in white clothes put Nana, my maternal great grandmother, on a stretcher. The siren makes no sound as the ambulance drives away.

I inwardly ask to take on all of my father's pain. I secretly ask to die so my father can live.

The family doctor, the physician who delivered me when I was born, walks out of the back door of the big house with his black leather medical bag. I silently watch his long stride as he approaches me. In a reassuring voice he says, "Your father is not going to die."

I feel calmer, but now I wonder if I may die instead because I made a bargain.

Alone on My Twelfth Birthday

I walk out the door to join my sister and our neighborhood friends playing in the yard. Everyone scatters and runs away when they see me coming. I look for them, but I can't find anyone to play with me. My grandmother tells me that my sister is playing a trick on me. When I hit my sister, my mother tells me to keep my hands to myself.

I try hard to follow all of my mother's rules. I don't contradict her even when I know she's wrong. I don't tell anyone that she smokes cigarettes with her friend, a seventh grade math teacher who lives across the street. I try not to do anything to embarrass my mother. I remember to be careful of what the neighbors think. I always respect my elders. After my grandmother's surgery, I never tell anyone that she had a hysterectomy, even though I don't know what that means. When I see a woman expecting a baby, I never say the word "pregnant."

* * *

Two years before, when I was in fifth grade, I watched a movie the school nurse showed to all the girls in my class. I learned that girls' bodies change so we can have babies when we grow up. At the end of the school day, I race home to share this newsflash with my mother and sister.

* * *

On my twelfth birthday my father is working late at the store. I'm home with my mother and my sister. At

Alone on My Twelfth Birthday

suppertime I walk into the kitchen. My mother and sister stand at the back door with their coats on ready to leave the house. I'm surprised to hear my mother say to me, "You don't mind if we go the movies to see "Whatever Happened to Baby Jane." You're too young to come with us. Besides, you have a sore throat. Your father will be home at 9:30."

I stare at the closed kitchen door. I know what I have to do. I open a package of Hostess cupcakes. I put a single candle in one chocolate cupcake with cream in the middle and a white squiggle on top. I light the candle. I have a distinct feeling that I'm not alone. I sing "Happy Birthday" to myself.

I tell myself that I am strong. I am independent and self-sufficient. I keep all my feelings and thoughts to myself. I talk only about good things and never say or think anything bad about anyone. I never complain no matter how hard I try or how much I hurt.

On my twelfth birthday, when I celebrate myself, I don't know yet that my sore throat is the beginning of a mystery illness that keeps me home from seventh grade for several months.

A Special Friendship

After school on the last day of junior high, I gather with a group of girls on the sidewalk in front of the school building. We eighth-grade graduates chat for the last time before dispersing for summer vacation. One classmate tells us that the science teacher, Mrs. Delaney, is upset and crying because none of the students said goodbye to her.

I go back inside the school with four of my friends. We march up the stairs and enter the science classroom. We don't see Mrs. Delaney, but we detect a faint sound coming from the walk-in closet. We call out the teacher's name. Sniffling, she meekly exits the closet and talks to us. We thank the science teacher and wish her a wonderful summer vacation.

* * *

I invite my four friends to walk home with me to celebrate the last day of junior high school. A boy we don't recognize walks in the same direction a short distance in front of us. We purposely walk faster to catch up with the boy and introduce ourselves. He walks with us since he lives in the neighborhood one street over from me.

When we get home, one of my friends suggests calling the boy on the phone. We look up his number in the phone book. My friends tell me to make the phone call. With their encouragement, I bravely dial the boy's phone number.

A Special Friendship

I already know that the boy is a year behind me in school. When we talk, I find out that he's 12 years old. His thirteenth birthday is only a couple of weeks away. The boy has an older sister and a younger brother. His family and my family belong to the same church. His best friend is our paperboy. The boy talks about his father.

I curiously ask about his mother. He tells me that his mother is dead. I want to say something to comfort the boy, but I am silent. I cannot speak. I feel the boy's deep pain. I feel guilty for asking him about his mother. I feel responsible for making him sad on the last day of school. For the first time, I see darkness in the space that opens when I close my eyes.

Three months later I enter high school. At a freshman class assembly, I listen attentively to the vice-principal talk about class officers and Student Council. I learn a new word when he warns the students not to be "apathetic." The vice principal's speech about responsibility and leadership so inspires me that I decide to become a candidate for office in the student government.

I speak into a microphone for the first time when I stand on stage to deliver my campaign speech to the freshman class. My knees shake and my hands sweat. I forget to breathe. I exhale the last few words of my brief speech and gulp for air. I have no voice for now, but after the votes are tallied, I am elected a class officer.

A Special Friendship

At the end of freshman year, a friend invites me to my first boy-girl party, a Hawaiian luau hosted by my friend's younger sister. My friend and her sister have a surprise for me: someone I know is coming to the party. On the night of the luau, an invisible spark ignites a special friendship with the boy I had met and called on the phone one year before.

That summer the boy and I form a tightly knit group with several friends. We swim in the back-yard pool and play continual rounds of Hearts and rummy. We listen to a wide range of music from the Beatles and Sonny and Cher to the soundtracks of *The Sound of Music* and *My Fair Lady*. We are too young to drive so we walk for miles and miles.

My father complains that I spend too much time with my friends. When I'm not home, the boy visits with my mother. I find him at my house when I return from a two-week trip to Florida with my aunt and uncle, my grandparents, and my sister.

One day at my house, the boy is very sad because he misses his mother. I'm upset because I am unable to help my friend. He solemnly walks out the door, shuffles down the street and heads home. With teary eyes, I silently beg my mother for help. My mother tells me to get in the car. We drive down the street and catch up with the boy.

In the car on the way back home, the boy sits in the front seat next to me. My heart feels heavy but my head feels light. I see a picture in the space that opens when I

A Special Friendship

close my eyes. I float with my special friend in that space where I saw my first kaleidoscope. In my picture, the boy and I face one another with outstretched arms. We drift on our stomachs as we float in an ocean that has no water. I keep this vision a secret, even from the boy.

Early one sunny afternoon, the boy and I walk together down Summer Street. On the corner of Park Avenue, at the entrance to Our Lady of Mount Carmel, a religious society to which my family belongs, the boy holds my hand for the first time. Embarrassed, I let go.

Summer ends and marks the beginning of another school year. The boy tells me that he doesn't want to be friends with me anymore. I hide my true feelings from him, but I'm heartbroken to lose my special friend. I mope on the green couch in the kitchen and listen to music by The Lettermen. I play the song "Smile" over and over again because the lyrics seem to speak directly to me. I try not to look sad when my next-door neighbor walks in the back door. He looks at me, turns to my mother and asks, "What's wrong with her?"

She casually replies, "Oh, it's just puppy love. She'll get over it."

* * *

I want my mother to see me for who I am and to really and truly know me. But she doesn't ask me how I feel, so I don't explain my special friendship with the boy.

Keeping the Secret

At a high school assembly, the vice-principal talks to the senior class about a change in plans for the annual class trip to Washington, D.C. He cannot accommodate all the student travelers in one tour. He arranges for two separate trips: the first in February and the second in April. He asks for students to volunteer for the second tour but no one in the senior class wants to wait until April. He tells the students that he has no choice but to randomly divide the group into two sections. At the end of the assembly, a number of students approach the vice-principal. We volunteer to postpone our class trip to Washington, D.C., until April.

The first group leaves on their excursion in February. They return with mounds of photographs depicting historical sights and mischievous adventures. The second group anxiously anticipates their upcoming trip when the weather will be warmer and the cherry blossoms in bloom.

April arrives, but tragedy strikes. Dr. Martin Luther King, Jr. is assassinated. The nation mourns. The country suffers from shock, turmoil and unrest. The anger and pain of this devastating loss spill into the streets of Washington, D.C. Riots and looting break out in cities all over the country. The assassination of Robert Kennedy in June compounds the heartache.

* * *

Keeping the Secret

My sister graduates from junior college that year and immediately leaves for California. She tells me that she can't wait and won't be back for my upcoming high school graduation. After graduation, my friends spend a leisurely summer working on Cape Cod. Instead of joining them, I take college courses during the day and work in a restaurant at night. I plan to graduate from college in three years instead of four.

My freshman year of college, I rent a single bedroom in a house off campus and go home most weekends. Eventually my sister returns from California and lives at home with our parents. One morning, as my sister puts on her make-up, she asks to talk to me. She tells me that she broke up with her boyfriend. He is a married man and he deals drugs. She has come home to piece her life back together.

After this conversation with my sister, my mother stops me in the hallway. She demands to know what my sister has just said to me. I tell her what I know about the breakup with the married drug dealer. My mother presses, "Did she tell you *everything*?" I answer, "Yes, she told me everything." My mother blurts out, "She told you about the baby?"

The walls in the hallway close in on me. My heart pounds; my head explodes and my body goes limp.

* * *

Keeping the Secret

My mother and sister confess the whole story. In California, my sister's boyfriend endangers her life and jeopardizes the life of the baby. In a culture of free love and hallucinogenic drugs, he tries to abort the unborn child. After a lengthy hospital stay, they move with the baby from California to Massachusetts. When the baby is two months old, my sister leaves the infant and the boyfriend and moves back home. The boyfriend gives the baby to his parents to raise as their own child.

I ask if my father knows about the baby. My mother emphatically states that he knows nothing about this dilemma. I plead with my mother and sister to tell my father everything. My mother warns me that I am never to tell my father the truth. If I do, she says she will never forgive me. She vows to hold me responsible for the breakup of her marriage if I ever tell my father about the baby.

* * *

My mother freely admits that she is spoiled. Her father and two older brothers, and now her husband, comply with all her wishes and satisfy all her needs. The caption in my mother's high school yearbook, *Tatler*, describes her perfect hair and perfect nails. She fixates on appearances and on the opinions of others. She occasionally smokes cigarettes and fears that her parents, brothers and husband will find out. My mother takes pride in being held in high esteem. She finds comfort in her religious belief that she is saved from damnation.

Keeping the Secret

* * *

My boyfriend, who I met when I was 15, is the one person in whom I confide. I anguish over my obligation to hide the truth from my father. My boyfriend reminds me that I am strong and that I have done nothing wrong. He is committed to me and pledges his love and support. He asks me to marry him in two years when he graduates from college.

* * *

One evening when I'm home from college on semester break, my boyfriend's family invites me to their house for dinner. I'm about to leave when my mother confronts me at the back door. She points to a kitchen chair and harshly commands, "Sit there. You're not going anywhere." I am stunned but I robotically obey. My sister and my father walk into the kitchen and stand with my mother.

My uncle, one of my mother's older brothers, storms through the back door and into the kitchen. In a rage, he accuses me of making my mother miserable. He blames me for causing her depression. My body convulses, and I break into tears. My uncle physically yanks the engagement ring off my finger and violently throws it across the room. With swollen eyes, I implore my mother and sister to tell the truth. They stand side by side in a silent conspiracy, along with my unwitting father, and condone my uncle's tirade. This unwarranted cruelty marks the onset of my bouts with prolonged, well-concealed depression.

Keeping the Secret

In the spring semester I stay at college most weekends. My boyfriend and I are at the park playing Frisbee. The circular disc flies over my head and out of my reach. I race toward the pond to retrieve the errant Frisbee. As I get closer to the water, I slow my steps to focus on a large object floating on the surface. Minutes later, the police, medics and firemen arrive to remove the dead body.

I long for a safe refuge. My boyfriend drives me home. At the front door, my father tells me that I may come in but my boyfriend is not welcome here. I solemnly turn from my father to walk away with my boyfriend, but he persuades me to go into the house to get some rest.

In the weeks that follow I attend college classes and walk straight home to my single, rented bedroom in a house off campus. One day, taking a shortcut through a vacant lot, I see a friend approach on the same path. Exuberant, she locks her arm in mine and says, "Where have you been? You're coming home with me."

For three days I stay in the dormitory apartment, affectionately remembered as B-11, with my three best friends from college. Cocooned in this safe haven, surrounded with love, I never say a word about my family troubles.

* * *

My sister always parks her GTO on the street in front of our house. One day she notices that her car is gone and breaks the news to my parents. My mother calls her brother who comes right over. My uncle is about to call the police when the doorbell rings. My father opens the front door. A stranger tells my father that he knows what happened to my sister's car.

Standing in the living room, the man explains to my parents, my sister, my uncle and me that my sister's former boyfriend has her car. This man's wife has betrayed him with the married drug dealer, the father of the baby my sister abandoned. He loves his wife and wants her back. He insists that my sister knows where to find her old boyfriend. The stranger points at my sister and says, "She had his baby."

My stunned father glares at my sister and hesitantly asks, "Is this true? Did you have a baby?"

I hold my breath and wait to hear the truthful answer. My heart pounds and my body shakes. I desperately want to be vindicated. I yearn to be released from my mother's tenacious hold and for my father to know the truth. And, I want this baby, my niece, in my life.

With vacant eyes, my sister turns to my father and resolutely answers, "No."

* * *

My mother and sister come to see me only once when I'm in college. Unexpected, they arrive late one afternoon in my sophomore year. My mother sharply asks, "How much money do you have in your bank account?"

Keeping the Secret

I have a savings account that my grandparents opened for me when I was ten years old. I have never made a withdrawal from this account. I pay my bills from the money I earn and put all my extra money into this account.

I tell my mother that I have almost two thousand dollars in savings. She orders me to go to the bank, withdraw all of my money and give it to my sister. She tells me not to tell my father about this visit. I follow her orders and ask no questions. I feel the heaviness of the compounding secrets I must keep from my father.

That spring, my sister and I stand next to her Super Beetle parked in the street in front of our house. An open letter sits on the front seat of her car. She hands me the letter and tells me that her child's grandparents, the acting parents, are blackmailing her. The letter is another demand for more money and new clothing. The grandparents threaten to tell my father about the child if my sister does not comply with their demands.

* * *

My intermittent depression worsens as the family predicament becomes more complex. I seek medical help for my illness, but the doctor tells me that I'm too young to be depressed. At the end of the semester, I plan a three-week road trip to California with my college roommate. She is my sister's friend and knows about my family situation, but she has concerns of her own. In the last two years, four of her five siblings have died: murder, suicide, a car accident and complications from a medical condition having caused these untimely deaths.

My roommate and I arrive in California and stay longer than we originally plan. We get jobs and rent an apartment for the summer. My boyfriend calls me and painfully asks why I'm deserting him. I cannot find the words to explain. I receive a letter from my uncle's wife. She writes, "How can you do this to us?" I throw the letter away.

In September I return from California. I rent an apartment off campus and begin the semester as a student teacher in a kindergarten classroom.

That fall my mother's father dies. The boyfriend I left behind comes to the funeral parlor. I melt when I see him, the first time since I'd left for California in late spring. My grandfather had been the only person in my family who had encouraged us to stay together. I hear him say to me in broken English, "He's a good boy. Marry him."

The Garden

In the crowded apartment above the flower shop, my fiancé and I gather around the television with college friends. Tension mounts as we listen fretfully to the numbers drawn by lottery. There are no student deferments. Now a college senior, my fiancé, my boyfriend from high school, draws a low number.

Six months later my slim, physically fit fiancé returns from Texas where he has been in basic training with the Air Force Reserves. In the car on the way home from the airport, I tell him my sad news.

The next day we drive to New York City for my 26-year-old cousin's funeral. She died of a stroke, a consequence of her battle with anorexia. At her funeral, my cousin's elderly aunt has a heart attack and dies.

* * *

My family is closely connected to both the Saint Joseph Society and Our Lady of Mount Carmel Society. I attend many church breakfasts, family gatherings and community events with members from each of these organizations. My bridal shower is held in Saint Joseph School's auditorium. My fiancé celebrates his stag party with his friends and relatives at Mount Carmel Hall.

Our wedding ceremony takes place at Saint Patrick Church, my hometown parish where I was baptized and confirmed. On the day of my confirmation I donned the name of the saint on a prayer card that my beloved teacher, Sister Mary Amelda, gave to me when I was in kindergarten. When I see the name Theresa on my confirmation certificate, I tell my mother that the spelling is Teresa, without an "h."

* * *

As a child I often pictured myself dressed in a floor-length habit. In my child vision, large wooden beads dangle from my waist and hide in the cavernous folds of dark fabric that fall to the floor. A swishy veil covers my bald head, and a hard, white band squeezes my face so tightly that it looks puffy.

In my child imagination I live in a brick convent with cement steps that lead to the front door. The sisters receive guests in the entryway, but there is no furniture. In the hallway each door opens into a room with a single bed. There's no carpeting anywhere; all the floors are bare. When I walk the long corridor in this prayer-filled house I hear the hollow echo of my footsteps, unaware that one day the labyrinth of life might allow me to discover a hidden connection with Teresa of Ávila.

* * *

I celebrated my confirmation day at a fashionable restaurant with all the women in my family: my mother, my grandmother, my aunt and my sister. On our wedding day the reception is held at the same restaurant, the Mountain Laurel, located diagonally across the street from the ball field behind my house.

The Garden

Before we marry, I tell my fiancé about my special friendship with the boy. I explain that I have dreams about him and that I inwardly communicate with him in the space that opens when I close my eyes. I innocently describe my secret vision in which the boy and I float in an ocean with no water. Desperately hoping to alleviate my interior anguish, I ask my fiancé to accept me as I am and to be a friend to me.

On my wedding day, as my father walks me down the aisle, a powerful presence overcomes me, a burning love that fires up inside of me. In that space, I see the boy. In that moment I fleetingly wonder, "What am I doing?" But with a joyful heart, devoted to the man I have chosen to love, I immediately erase this passing thought from my mind.

A week after our wedding, when my husband finishes summer camp with the Air Force Reserves, we drive to Ogunquit, on the coast of Maine, for our honeymoon. After breakfast one sunlit morning, a man in the front yard of Barbara Dean's, a local restaurant, invites me to walk with him to look at the flowers. He takes me on a private tour of the grounds. He explains to me how he cares for the various flowers in the garden and shows me the hearty bushes and trimmed trees. He tells me that he weeds and maintains the extensive garden himself.

I tell the gardener that my husband and I are newlyweds. He reaches into his shirt pocket and takes out a prayer

The Garden

card. On the front of the prayer card is a picture of a colorful flower garden. He hands the prayer card to me and says, "God will always be with you."

Talking with this gardener reminds me of an incident from my childhood. On the cement walkway next to the garden in the side yard of the big house above the family store, I tag along with my older cousin and three of his friends. I like to play basketball and football with them. My cousin jokingly tells his younger friend that I can beat him up. Without warning, my cousin's friend pushes me down onto the rough sidewalk. My bloody knee gets badly infected and takes an unusually long time to heal.

* * *

Fifty years later my husband and I take my uncle out to dinner at a family restaurant in our hometown. As we walk by a married couple sitting in a booth, the man calls out to my uncle. When the woman sees me, she jumps out of her seat and lovingly embraces me. She excitedly repeats my first and maiden names, three times in a row.

This woman is my friend who hosted the Hawaiian luau in high school. An experienced nurse, she had voluntarily cared for my mother, sixteen years earlier, when she was hospitalized with pancreatic cancer. When the doctors wouldn't answer my questions about my mother's condition, this friend had gently told me that my mother wasn't going home and would die in the hospital.

The Garden

My friend's husband explains to us that he is preparing for a kidney transplant in one week so he can't shake our hands or get too close. Remarkably, this man is also a longtime lung transplant recipient and survivor. After his life-saving surgery in 2000, he became a counselor for other transplant patients. He works as a volunteer for the American Lung Association.

As we talk, my friend's husband mentions an incident from our youth that I remember well. When we were children, he was the boy who had pushed me down on the sidewalk next to the garden at the big house, resulting in the subsequent injury that had taken so long to heal.

As we discuss the upcoming transplant, the memory of my childhood injury echoes back to me in concentric circles. Healing, like ripples from a pebble that falls into a still lake, moves through time and space.

I think of my father and the little red berry bush that he grew from a seed. He regularly transplanted the whisper of life back into the earth to sustain its existence. Now, transplantation offers my friend and her husband a pathway to activate the human body's inner potential to sustain life. My friends' eyes tell me that their love nourishes and grounds them on the earth. Like all living things, they carry within their nature a unique path to center.

My Inner Secret

When I run home from the ball field at the top of the hill behind my house, I imagine that red-eyed animals, much bigger than rabbits, snap at my heels. When I walk home from school on the dirt road alongside the ball field, I imagine that someone walks behind me to protect me. Sometimes I pivot around really fast to take this imaginary person by surprise. I'm sure that if I try hard enough, I will see this invisible protector with my own eyes.

I often sit at the edge of my bed and gaze out the window into my backyard. When I'm by myself, I picture the snapping animals with red eyes and simultaneously feel the presence of my imaginary companion.

One day, as I sit at the foot of my bed and stare out my bedroom window, I hear a whirring sound. In the distance I see a helicopter fly toward my house. Mesmerized, I watch the whirlybird land in my backyard. With two men sitting in the cockpit, the helicopter rests on the ground for just a minute. Then, light as air, the flying machine rises up from the ground and takes off in the direction of the ball field.

As I watch the propeller blades rotate around and around, I feel the earth vibrate deep inside of me. Long after the helicopter is out of sight, I continue to hear a whirring, like the echo from a seashell held close to the ear. This whirring, what I have come to believe is the earth's natural vibration, stays with me throughout my life.

* * *

My Inner Secret

When I call the boy on the last day of school in eighth grade, I feel a stirring deep inside of me when he tells me that his mother is dead. My heart beats faster and my hands sweat. I close my eyes and instantly go to that place where I see my first kaleidoscope. This time, instead of seeing bright colors and freely moving patterns, I see darkness. I met the boy just an hour ago, but I feel his intense pain as if I've known him all my life. This indescribable anguish that I feel draws me in close to the boy.

I imagine the words I want to say to comfort him but I emit no sound. I have no voice. From within I feel a vibration and hear a soothing whirring sound. In a dreamy vision, light as air, I surmount the earthly world and float endlessly in my boundless interior sanctuary.

* * *

As a child I never doubted that my imaginary kaleidoscope was real. The world I experienced inside of me and the world I saw with my physical eyes were one and the same. I reveled in the stirrings that came about naturally when I gazed out of my bedroom window, walked in the woods or looked up into the sky. Melodic sounds and artistic renderings also prompted this comforting sense of dawning.

* * *

In my late teens, when my family life fractures, I retreat into the safety of my inner world. Here I create a space where I am loved and accepted as I am. In my inward sanctuary I imagine that the boy is the only one who understands me. Without words, we talk about friendship, forgiveness, surrender and divine love.

In my early twenties this interior communication, my inner secret, becomes a daily practice. I attribute my gift of inner knowingness to the boy. In my imagination he is a conduit who transfers spiritual information to me. I don't yet see that I may have a role in deciphering my own inner truths.

The boy's constant inner presence both comforts and torments me. I never try to contact him in person, but I become obsessed with my constant search for him. I am compelled to look for him, day and night, wherever I am. I struggle with this relentless, driving force that never lets me rest. I seriously question my own sanity but I'm sure that one day, I'll find the boy.

For years I harbor my guarded inner secret. I live in constant fear that my concealed interior life will be exposed and hope that no one, not even my husband, will ever suspect the depth of my baffling inner conflict. I no longer have the security of the child who coexisted harmoniously in both worlds. My two worlds are no longer one and the same. I now live a chaotic, double existence: a public life that the world sees on the outside and a secret, hidden life in a world that only I see from the inside.

I long for a restful place of reconciliation between these two seemingly opposite worlds, my physical existence and my spiritual existence. In the labyrinth of life, that tranquil place is my center, my true home.

My Inner Secret

* * *

The annual church fair in our hometown is walking distance from our new home. The blacktop parking lot behind the church is a temporary site for games of chance, food booths and carnival rides. I weave through the crowd. I catch a glimpse of a man's profile as he works inside a ticket booth. I gasp aloud. I have not seen the boy in five years.

The man in the booth curiously asks, "Do I know you?"

Disheartened I reply, "I'm sorry. You look like someone I used to know."

* * *

As a child, I walk barefoot from my house to the familiar grounds of Our Lady of Mount Carmel. I pass three neighboring houses, cross the street, slip between the side yards of the next two houses, climb over the fence and walk through the cemetery. The entrance to Mount Carmel is a short block ahead.

* * *

The highlight of the summer is the annual Our Lady of Mount Carmel Italian Festival. Carnival workers and volunteers from Mount Carmel Society set up for the traditional gala. Colorful overhead lights line the street that leads to the entrance of the park. The empty field transforms into a lively celebration – a playground of food, music, games and rides.

Sweet and pungent smells fill the air. Food booths line the outer brick wall of Mount Carmel Hall. Players of all ages, eager to win prizes, crowd the rows of games. Flashing lights, spinning wheels and multi-colored banners adorn the cubicles. The dance band takes center stage on the raised pavilion. The grassy field beyond is outfitted for the fireworks extravaganza while the fire department stands by in full regalia.

* * *

At the feast I embrace a friend from the tightly knit group of teenagers that had formed eight summers before. He introduces me to his wife and child.

After the fireworks that night, I sit with my husband and our troop of friends in folding chairs at a long banquet table under the stars. The boy's best friend, the paperboy from my childhood, is with his wife. The host of the Hawaiian luau in high school is with her husband, the boy who pushed me down onto the sidewalk near the garden at the big house. Her sister, the friend who invited me to the luau, is with her husband. His uncle owns the dairy bar where I once worked with several of my high school friends. My cousin who drove me to the church on my wedding day is seated with his wife, his childhood girlfriend from Saint Joseph School.

When the conversation inevitably turns to one friend who is not at the festival, my heart aches with fear and anxiety. Usually the last to leave a party, I feel an urgent need to flee. On that balmy summer night, I walk five miles alone in the dark to the safety of home.

The First Encounter

Family and friends arrive at the surprise college graduation party and fill our modest ranch house to capacity. The lively celebration catches me off guard. Before I officially graduate, I must complete three hectic weeks of student teaching in a sixth grade classroom at a school an hour away from home. When the school year ends, I plan to spend carefree summer days relaxing with my close friend who has recently graduated from college and moved back to our hometown. This friend introduced me to my husband when we were in high school.

* * *

On a hot summer day, my friend and I pack a lunch and leisurely drive the hour to a town beach. After a refreshing swim, we lazily stretch out on oversized towels and bask in the sun.

Suddenly, a park official speaks into a megaphone and rouses us with his thunderous voice. He urgently asks for strong swimmers to come forward. Away from the megaphone, he hurriedly explains the mission to a cluster of volunteers. The final recruits follow him to an ordinarily off-limits part of the reservoir closed to swimmers. Their troublesome task is to find a man who fell into the depths of the reservoir and disappeared.

* * *

In the fall I compete with a multitude of qualified applicants for a handful of full-time teaching positions.

The First Encounter

Resigned to working part-time, I settle into my flexible role as a substitute teacher. I occasionally work at the neighborhood parochial school that shares the blacktop parking lot behind the church where the fair comes to life every summer. Mostly I substitute teach at various public schools scattered throughout my hometown.

As the winter holidays approach, I stroll down the wide walkway of the local shopping mall. A portrait artist paints at his easel in the heavily trafficked center of the mall. In the space that opens when I close my eyes, I see the thirteen-year-old boy. He sits next to me at the picnic table in my backyard on a hot summer day. Side by side, we color the blank spaces inside the heavy black lines of the open coloring book. At the bottom of the left-hand page, below his colorful picture, I print in blue crayon, "Chuck the Artist."

* * *

For years I harbor my inner secret, the interior voice. I struggle with the driving force that compels me to constantly search for the boy. When I unexpectedly see him painting portraits at the mall, I am shocked. Anxiety-stricken and clenched with fear, I try to appear calm as I casually approach the artist. I invite him to come to our house for dinner.

My husband and I welcome the artist into our home. After dinner, the artist talks openly to me about the spiritual path he follows. He speaks extensively about spiritual masters, contemplation, soul travel and the journey back "home." Attentively listening to his talk of illumination, I experience a nostalgic yearning. When he speaks about divine love, I am acutely aware of a powerful surge of energy that wells up from a fountain deep inside of me.

I'm too shy to divulge my inner secret to the artist. I'm embarrassed to tell him of the connection I've felt with him since the first day we met when he told me that his mother had died. When he again shares about divine love, I unearth the courage to imperceptibly mouth the unspoken words, "I love you divinely."

* * *

On holiday, the artist stays with his sister, who belongs to my church and regularly serves on committees with me. She lives in the same neighborhood as one of my high school friends. At a gathering of classmates at this friend's house one night, I convince the group to walk with me to visit the artist at his sister's home. On the way back, I ask one of my friends if she feels the wave of love and peace that emanates from the artist. I am perplexed when she skeptically looks at me and flatly replies, "No."

Before returning to his home in Florida, the artist gives me several books. I don't read any of them. Instead of reading books, I choose to discover my own spiritual truth for myself, through my own efforts. I give all of the books to a mutual friend.

The First Encounter

On my own, I practice the spiritual exercises that the artist has described to me. With great resolve, I relax in an upright position on the gold living-room carpet etched with a high school friend's accidental cigarette burn. I enter the space that opens when I close my eyes, the place where I see the kaleidoscope of my childhood.

Go Home

Today is my first day substitute teaching for a three-month term in a third-grade classroom. Memories surface as I creep along the driveway on the right side of the school and park my car behind the building. This elementary school is my old junior high school. In my mother's day, it was her high school.

I get out of the car and focus on the overgrown basketball court next to the parking lot. In my memory I see my uncle perform his repetitive race as referee from one end of this basketball court to the other. On a balmy summer night long ago, moths swarm in the beams of artificial light that illumine the glossy, competitive athletes. Barefoot, I climb up on the wooden bleachers and watch my uncle ref the game.

* * *

Musing, I enter the homeroom where I will teach for the next three months. Directly above me on the second floor is the science classroom where Mrs. Delaney cried because none of her eighth-grade students said goodbye to her on the last day of school. The room next door to me is my seventh grade math classroom. I remember struggling, on my own, to catch up with the rest of the class when I was absent from school for three months that year. In the now third-grade classroom, I remember the family friend who taught seventh-grade math in this same room over a decade ago.

Go Home

I gaze out of the front window of the empty classroom. I see the sidewalk where I chatted with my friends on the last day of school in eighth grade. I see myself go back into the building with my friends to console Mrs. Delaney. I relive walking home with my friends and meeting the boy.

* * *

I feel comfortable and confident teaching in the third-grade classroom. I'm quite fond of all the children. One morning, with only one month left to spend with them before my long-term substitute teaching assignment ends, a man I don't know opens the door and walks into the classroom. The children screech with delight and dart toward him. Surrounded by the excited third graders, he tells his students that he will be back to school tomorrow.

* * *

After the abrupt separation from the third graders, I turn my attention to the spiritual exercises that the artist described to me when he visited. Sitting quietly on the gold carpet on my living-room floor, I see vivid pictures and hear a soothing voice in the space that opens when I close my eyes.

* * *

I fall back into the flexible role of substitute teaching at various schools on short notice. One morning a full-time teacher carries a large wicker basket into the teachers' room. I take home the tiniest of the seven writhing puppies, a feisty black male with brown markings. I name him Teddy.

Every day when I walk Teddy, I pass by a horse farm near our neighborhood. In a dreamy state, I stare at the horses that graze and frolic in the pasture. When I talk to my husband about getting a horse, he tells me that dreams are meant to come true. My first horse is a gentle palomino named Schaeffer. On horseback, I am free to explore winding trails through the woods and dirt roads in the tobacco and potato fields in my hometown.

* * *

On the night before Thanksgiving, I receive an unexpected phone call. The principal of a parochial school introduces herself. She tells me that she needs a math and science teacher for all the students in grades five, six, seven and eight. On Friday, the day after Thanksgiving, I drive 12 miles from home to an interview at a school I didn't know existed. On Monday, my twenty-fourth birthday, I celebrate my first day of employment as a full-time teacher.

The principal lives in the convent next to the school. At home one winter night, she notices that the light in my classroom is still on. She slips into the school and walks quietly up the stairs to the second floor. She glides into the classroom and finds me working at my desk. She glances down at the foot-high stack of tests and homework papers that I am grading and furrows her brow. Sister Mary Gerald rhetorically asks, "What are you doing here so late?"

In one smooth motion, she securely seizes the mound of papers with her graceful hands. With outstretched arms, she raises the load to eye-level. She hesitates for one breathtaking moment then theatrically releases the mountain of work into the awaiting circular wastebasket on the floor next to my desk. Signifying the completion of a task, she swipes her open hands against one another twice. Sister Mary Gerald looks at me intently and commands in a gentle voice, "Go home."

A New Life

One Sunday morning after reading the real estate section of *The Hartford Courant*, my husband declares, "We're going for a ride."

We drive to the town where I swam and basked in the sun with my friend on the day the man fell into the reservoir. My husband stops the car on a winding country road in the middle of the woods. Keeping his anticipation in check, he points out the beaver pond on the five-acre parcel of land with a secluded house.

* * *

We camp out in the empty house every weekend for the next two months. Isolated in the middle of the woods, I feel far away from civilization. We rip out tattered wall-to-wall carpeting, strip and refinish dreary kitchen cabinets, wax dull floors and spray cleaning agents until the whole house shines. At night we wearily roll out our sleeping bags on the bare living room floor. Before I drift off to sleep, I visualize the distance from this house to the school where I teach. I know that the lengthy commute is unfeasible.

Potential homebuyers tour our first home, our modest ranch house, but it's still on the market. As we approach our tentative moving date, my ambivalent feelings increase. I reluctantly give Sister Mary Gerald my resignation.

As soon as I stop teaching school, I catch a persistent flu that doesn't seem to go away. I eat only graham crackers and mashed potatoes. After three weeks of constant illness,

A New Life

my friend lightheartedly remarks, "I don't think you have the flu."

Despite my medical history and the doctor's warning that I may have difficulty conceiving a child, the test results are positive.

No longer teaching school, I can't picture myself at home with a new baby in a remote town far from my friends and family. My husband and I agree to sell the isolated house with five acres of land and a beaver pond. For several months we carry two mortgages and hope that the newly purchased house will sell first. We are stunned when both houses sell in the same week. Honoring the real estate contracts we have signed, we scramble to find a new place to live.

On Memorial Day weekend, we move into a two-story house one town away from our modest ranch house.

* * *

That fall my husband and I go to a birthday party for my cousin who drove me to the church on my wedding day. He and his wife live in a new house in the neighborhood where I grew up. The houses across the street from their Cape-style dwelling are much older. As a barefoot child, I slipped between these established houses, climbed over a fence and walked through the cemetery to get to Our Lady of Mount Carmel.

* * *

A New Life

At my cousin's birthday party, I compete in a lively game of ping-pong. On my hands and knees, I crawl under the length of the table to retrieve an errant ball. That night, when my husband and I get home from the party, he immediately falls asleep. Finally ready for sleep myself, I stop abruptly just short of the bed and gasp.

Late the next night, in the delivery room, I cradle our newborn daughter in my arms. With my eyes wide open, I float to that place where I meet the boy.

The next morning our childbirth instructor comes into our room on the maternity floor. She thoughtfully brings two gifts, a frothy vanilla milkshake and a book of poignant poems about motherhood. This nurse, a dedicated midwife, is the friend who invited me to her sister's Hawaiian luau in high school.

False Accusations Against My Father

In the musty basement of the house where I live with my parents and my sister, I find two stacks of books secured with butcher's twine tied in a corned-beef knot – books on accounting, law, taxes and business management. Curious, I show them to my father. He tells me the story behind these textbooks that he bought when I was a baby.

* * *

The oldest son of nine surviving children, my father worked in the family business, a meat and grocery store, since he was a boy. Even though he had no choice but to work in the store, he desperately tried to stay in school. He managed to finish seventh grade, but the next year my father's father demanded that he quit school and work in the store full-time.

One day my father snuck out of the store. Fearful yet determined, he rode his dilapidated bicycle to school. During math, his favorite subject, his disdainful father barged into the classroom and yanked him out of his chair, marching him out of the classroom and forcing him to go back to work in the store. In addition to the corporal punishment, my paternal grandfather destroyed my father's hand-assembled bike and every recreational plaything that he owned.

* * *

After I was born, my father enrolled in night school to earn his GED (General Educational Development) certificate, the equivalent of a high school diploma. On school nights, he parked his car in a nearby lot and walked to school. In class one night, two uniformed policemen burst into the classroom. They grabbed my father by his arms, lifted him out of his chair and removed him from the classroom. They put him in a cruiser and took him to the police station.

During the police interrogation, my father found out that he was accused of slashing the seats of a car parked in the lot near the school. The police told my father that a witness saw him walk through the parking lot earlier that night.

Humiliated and expelled from school, my father tied up his textbooks with twine and buried them in the basement.

Two years later, a school administrator called him and apologized for expelling him from school. She also acknowledged the police mistake in accusing my father of committing a crime.

* * *

When my father told me why he was expelled from night school when I was a baby, it made me very sad. When he went on to tell me that one of his brothers had once beaten him with a broomstick for no reason, I was even more distressed. I wanted to comfort my father, but I didn't have the words. For many years I had frequent nightmares about the false accusations and unfair treatment that my father had endured.

False Accusations Against My Father

As I entered adulthood, the pain of my mother's betrayal, keeping the secret of my sister's pregnancy, exacerbated the unspeakable agony I felt in empathy with my father's heartache and suffering. False accusation became the fundamental trigger that initiated each major depression that has challenged my life.

* * *

My father, a business owner and expert meat-cutter, has a side business cleaning carpets. I stay up late, even on school nights, to help him clean area rugs on the raised, wooden platform in our basement. I also go with him on jobs to clean wall-to-wall carpets in customers' homes.

After college, when teaching jobs are scarce, I help my father clean carpets in addition to working as a substitute teacher. One day my father asks me to help him start a new business, P & J Carpet Care. I concentrate on the business for a year, but I cut back on working with my father when I unexpectedly fall into a full-time teaching position at a parochial school. When I resign from that job and subsequently give birth to my first daughter, I rarely clean carpets with my father anymore.

* * *

When my daughter is two months old, Sister Mary Gerald, the school principal, once again calls me unexpectedly. She tells me about the string of teachers who she had hired to replace me since I stopped teaching at the parochial school. One by one, each of the newly employed teachers had quit.

As she speaks, I am mindful of another secret I must keep. The younger nuns refer to one of the parish priests as Father Gorgeous. I know this man because he occasionally visits with the children at school. Prior to giving my first resignation to Sister Mary Gerald, I saw him walk through the mall in my hometown where the artist painted portraits. The priest held hands with a woman who I recognized, the friend of a friend.

On a Monday in December, as a favor to the school principal, I resume my full-time job teaching math and science to fifth, sixth, seventh and eighth graders. Caught in an awkward situation, I deliberately avoid the young priest and any conversation regarding him.

* * *

School is out of session for the summer. I'm home with my daughter, playing on the deep blue carpet in the empty living room. Through the front picture window I see a state trooper drive up our long driveway. With the baby in my arms, I inquisitively greet the tall, physically fit officer in my front yard.

He questions, "Do you own the horse that's running loose and causing traffic problems?"

I tell him that it's not my horse, but probably my next-door neighbor's horse that's on the loose. The officer casually glances toward my neighbor's house. He is reluctant to leave my front yard.

I ask the state trooper, "What are you better at, catching horses or watching babies?"

Standing next to the spot where we eventually plant the bush my father grew from a little red berry, the officer gently reaches for my daughter, holds her in his arms and responds, "You catch the horse. I'll watch the baby."

* * *

One Wednesday that summer, on my father's regular day off from the supermarket where he now works, he and I walk with my daughter in her stroller. He pushes the baby carriage along the sidewalk in front of my house. He passes through the gate and enters the pool area. I am silent when my father humbly says to me, "Not all families are as close as we are."

Two weeks later, in the middle of July, my mother calls to say that my father is on a carpet job. My uncle is with him to help. She tells me that when my father finishes work for the day, they are coming to see the baby.

Several hours later I learn that my father is in the emergency room at the local hospital. The doctors diagnose him with a gall bladder attack. I wait for the babysitter to arrive then drive to the emergency room to be with him.

* * *

False Accusations Against My Father

At the hospital I find my father in excruciating pain. He says the pain started when he and my uncle arrived at the customer's house to clean the carpets. After physically exerting and distressing himself for two hours, my uncle drove him to the emergency room. The doctors admitted my father to the hospital and told him he would be moved upstairs when a bed became available.

* * *

I stand by my father's side as he lays on the bed in the emergency room. His contorted body and facial grimace tell me that his pain is unbearable. I sense that he has something on his mind. When he asks me to finish the carpet-cleaning job that he started that morning, I know I am still my father's helper.

Before I turn to leave the room, for the first time in my life, I hear my father say, "I love you."

Shaken, I tell him that I love him, too. I assure him that I will be back as soon as I finish the job.

In a weak voice my father utters the words, "I hope I don't die."

* * *

After I finish cleaning the carpets, I thank the customer for her patience and load the carpet equipment into my father's station wagon. I go home to check on my daughter and take a shower. I'm ready to walk out the door to go back to the hospital when the phone rings.

False Accusations Against My Father

I answer the phone. I hear my sister say, "Daddy's heart stopped. You better come to the hospital right now."

In a daze, I recklessly speed back to the hospital. Through the clear glass inserts in the double doors, I see my father's lifeless body flopped on a metal table covered with bloodstained sheets. When the paddles are applied to his cut chest, I watch my father's body involuntarily leave the table.

The spent, young doctor exits through the double doors. I reach out to him, but he avoids my touch. He tells me not to enter the room where my father lays now. He vacantly states, "There's nothing I can do."

As he ambles down the corridor, I follow the doctor with my eyes. I feel a cold emptiness in the echo of his footsteps.

I later learn that the doctors misdiagnosed my father's medical condition. He died of an abdominal aortic aneurysm.

On the day of my father's burial, a low-flying crop-duster appears across the street from the funeral parlor. It reminds me that my father wanted to ride in a plane someday.

The Life in My Hands

I walk up the hill behind my house to meet my uncle at the ball field. At the practice session he shouts to me from the pitcher's mound, "Get out here, Pal, and show these boys how to play ball."

I take a batter's stance over home plate and choke up on the bat. My uncle pitches the ball and I get a hit. I move to my next position in center field. My uncle bats a ball high up into the air. I keep my eye on the ball and catch the pop fly. He bats another ball in my direction. This time I squat to capture the bouncy grounder with my gloved hand and protect it with my bare hand.

After the demonstration for the boys on the Little League team my uncle coaches, I stand next to the dugout where I'm not allowed to sit during their practice. When they play a real game, I disappear into the crowd on the sidelines or sit high up on the wooden bleachers.

My family says that I'm a tomboy but I just love to play sports. I don't like to play with dolls or get dressed up in frilly clothes. I'd rather challenge myself to run faster and throw the ball further. I'm comfortable with my natural physical strength and athletic ability.

I also like to work hard, especially when I can help my father. Sometimes I don't have enough strength, but he always lets me try to tackle heavy jobs anyway. When he planted new grass in our yard I wasn't strong enough to budge the metal hand roller that presses the grass seed firmly into the soil. To lighten the load, my father removed the cap from the holding tank and tipped the cumbersome piece of equipment onto its side. As I watched the weighty water flow out of the vessel, I eagerly anticipated my turn to push and pull the now manageable roller over the newly seeded lawn.

A butcher by trade, my father sometimes surprises me and brings home young animals from the "farm" on the outskirts of our hometown. He explains that I may play with the baby goat or lamb or calf for the afternoon, but he must always bring the animals back to the "farm" at the end of the day. I never question why.

When I have to be indoors I always find interesting ways to keep busy. I spend hours piecing together jigsaw puzzles. I decipher crosswords, word-fills and other tricky word games in the magazines I collect. I tie ropes into complex knots so I can untangle the tightly wadded masses. I make up my own "never-ending" long division problems and solve them just for fun.

I do not feel well when I celebrate my twelfth birthday. In addition to my sore throat I develop a persistent low-grade fever, respiratory congestion and fatigue. I have aches and pains all over my body. I discover that I can predict the weather because the joints in my fingers hurt just before it starts to rain. Sometimes my knees hurt so badly that I cry myself to sleep at night. My mother tells me that I have growing pains.

The Life in My Hands

My illness baffles our family doctor and mystifies my new specialist, a pediatrician in Springfield. Once when I was sick a man with a black medical bag came to our house. I was scared when he took out a sharp needle, a thick length of rubber band and some glass vials. He said he had to draw my blood to help the doctor find out what was wrong with me.

We soon learn that I'm anemic, but the iron deficiency doesn't explain all of my symptoms. I eat a lot of steak and drink a chocolate milkshake every day. I am repulsed when I accidentally find out that my mother blends a raw egg into each of my high-calorie beverages.

During the lengthy time I'm absent from school I especially look forward to company. One afternoon my cousin, the one I tried to surprise with his towel at the beach when I was four, comes to visit with his girlfriend. She notices that I like to keep busy and asks if I want to learn how to knit. As I sit next to her on the green couch, she teaches me to knit and purl with two sharpened pencils and a ball of ordinary kitchen string. After my cousin and his high-school girlfriend break up, I never see her again.

* * *

Many years later my cousin and his wife, who worked for my pediatrician when I was mysteriously ill in seventh grade, live in the same town as my husband, our children and me, the town where I plant the bush my father grew from a little red berry. When my daughters attend nursery school in the center of town, my cousin's wife is their teacher. Her older sister is married to her husband's older brother, also my cousin.

* * *

During my extended absence from school in seventh grade my principal decides that I don't need a tutor. He says that I won't have to make up any of the schoolwork assigned in my accelerated classes. But when I return to school in April, I quickly learn that my teachers expect me to catch up, on my own, to the academic level of my peers. I work extra hard to earn the grades I need to stay in this challenging program with my classmates.

* * *

A generation later, when my first-born daughter is 12 years old, she exhibits the same medical symptoms that I experienced when I was her age. At the onset of my daughter's illness, I am confined to bed rest. Over a period of three years, I have two back surgeries followed by two and a half years of physical therapy. Because of my immobility, I call upon friends and family members to take my daughter to her medical appointments. For two months I make weekly phone calls to the pediatrician's office to report my daughter's continual symptoms. One afternoon an irritated nurse picks up the phone and harshly retorts, "Stop calling this office. There is nothing clinically wrong with your child."

The Life in My Hands

One morning as I awaken from a dreamy sleep, I intuitively know that my daughter needs to see a rheumatologist. My dear friend, a hematologist, arranges for one of her colleagues to evaluate her. This friend, my mother and another dear friend, a nurse, bring her to the scheduled appointment.

A week later the specialist determines that my daughter has JRA, juvenile rheumatoid arthritis, and starts her on a regimen of medications. As I reflect upon this diagnosis I spiral back to when I was 12 years old. Now, after 27 years, I begin to comprehend the mystery illness that plagued me when I was in seventh grade.

* * *

In contrast to my confidence and trust in my physical prowess as a natural child athlete, I experience an awkward transition into early adolescence.

When I return to school after my extended illness, my mother occasionally picks me up at the end of the school day. As I get into the car one afternoon she points out one of my friends wearing nylon stockings and penny loafers with her sweater and skirt ensemble. My mother admiringly critiques, "I like her collegiate style."

Embarrassed, I look down at my cuffed, white cotton ankle socks. My mother doesn't allow me to wear nylon stockings. Four years later the classmate my mother admired that day became editor-in-chief of our high school yearbook, *Echo*.

The Life in My Hands

In seventh grade I sometimes get a ride to school with my neighbor, a math teacher. While I wait in her house one morning I notice a small, blue cardboard box. Curious I ask, "What are tampons?"

Caught off guard she answers, "When you get home from school today, you better ask your mother."

The summer after seventh grade, when I finish mowing a neighbor's lawn, the outspoken woman tells me that I need a brassiere. I walk home and inquisitively ask my mother, "What's a brassiere?"

My mother takes me shopping for my first bra. At suppertime she tells me to take the new purchase out of the shopping bag and show it to my father and sister. My sister laughs and says that my training bra looks like a garter belt. I am too embarrassed to ask what a garter belt is.

At the end of the summer, against my mother's orders, I use my sister's toxic-smelling chemical product to remove the hair on my legs. Satisfied with their smoothness, I rush to find my mother on the back porch. I proudly inform her of my landmark accomplishment in preparation for my first day of school in eighth grade. Disgruntled she says, "That's too bad. Now you'll have to keep it up for the rest of your life."

Almost two years later, at home after the last day of school in ninth grade, I fretfully explain to my sister that

I think I have cancer. She laughs and tells me that I have my period.

* * *

A month before my wedding a high school friend, now married to the brother of the boy who pushed me down next to the garden at the big house, advised me on birth control. Her gynecologist, now my doctor, fits me with an intrauterine device, a seemingly simple and harmless way to prevent pregnancy. From the time the IUD is inserted I have persistent cramps and frequent bleeding. When I ask the doctor to remove it, he tells me to give my body a chance to acclimate. After many uncomfortable months I again ask the doctor to remove the device. During the pelvic exam he tells me that the IUD is not there.

Certain that the foreign object is still in my body I change doctors. I ask the new gynecologist to remove the culprit. Like the last doctor, he doesn't see the device during the pelvic exam. He deduces that the IUD fell out and I just didn't notice it.

In spite of this physician's assumption I insist that the offensive contraption is still inside my body. The doctor dismisses my entreaty but decides to do a DNC to alleviate the bleeding. That afternoon, still drowsy from anesthesia for the uterine scraping, I anxiously ask the surgeon, "Did you remove the IUD?"

* * *

The Life in My Hands

In desperation I approach a third gynecologist. He listens and methodically evaluates my medical predicament. He determines that the IUD is still inside my body but has traveled outside of my uterus, perforating it. He notes that the seven DNC's and the scores of hormonal injections that I had endured over the previous two years were futile. He underscores the fact that I ovulate irregularly and infrequently.

After several more weeks, the gynecologist surgically removes the pestilent device from my body. At a follow-up conference in his office he mentions that the previous doctors made mistakes. He urges me to just let these mishaps go, for my own good. He then asks if I intend to have children at some point in the future. When I answer "yes," he informs me that my chance of ever getting pregnant is slim to none.

* * *

Our first daughter was nine months old when my father died. In the months that follow I privately drown in the depths of my own hopelessness. Relegated to a lifetime of knowing that I betrayed him, I am distraught that I will never have the chance to tell my father the truth about the baby my sister and my mother kept secret from him. He will never know that upon the birth of his abandoned, first-born grandchild, we became a family of five living generations.

* * *

The Life in My Hands

Three months after my father's death my sister's wedding takes place as originally planned. My mother does not want to live alone. She moves into a newly constructed in-law apartment attached to our home. Before she entirely leaves the family house, I dig up the bush that my father grew from a little red berry and plant the bush, now 23 years old, in my own front yard.

* * *

One morning while I'm home with my daughter I suffer severe abdominal cramps and bleeding. I'm used to difficult menstrual cycles but I know that something atypical is happening inside my body. In the next hour the pain becomes incapacitating and the hemorrhaging is profuse. I suddenly feel my body open as if expelling a massive blood clot. I instinctively catch the warm mass in my hands as it emerges from my body.

Still grief-stricken over my father's sudden death, I now mourn the loss of my unborn baby. In despair I begin to suffer frequent, debilitating migraine headaches that will continue to plague me for the next 20 years. To cope I turn inward to center, to that secret place where I talk to the boy.

* * *

The following school year I give Sister Mary Gerald, my principal, my resignation for the second time. Expecting another baby, I am confined to bed rest for the last month of my pregnancy. Accustomed to episodes of false labor, I wait to call my obstetrician until I am sure that the labor is real.

At the hospital a female resident checks the fetal monitor and concludes that I am not ready to deliver the baby. I logically explain to the young woman that I am a mother. I know my body, and I am certain that my baby's birth is imminent.

The arrogant resident dismisses my view of the progress of my labor and trusts the faulty fetal monitor. She gives me an ultimatum: either I go home, a 25-minute drive from the hospital, or she injects me with morphine and sends me to an empty hospital room upstairs to rest.

My husband tells me that he's tired and going home to get some sleep. Downtrodden, I ultimately have no choice but to succumb to the demands of this tyrannical resident.

Drugged with morphine and alone in an isolated hospital room, my water breaks. I ring for a nurse and panic when he tells me that he can't bring me downstairs to a delivery room. He says that a doctor from Obstetrics must first come upstairs to evaluate me. When the male nurse calls for assistance from Obstetrics, the female resident takes her time to respond.

Drenched in amniotic fluid and contorted by severe uterine contractions, I roll off the hospital bed and onto the floor. I crawl to a bedside table and yank on the telephone cord. When the phone crashes to the floor I hysterically dial home. My husband finally answers the phone and tells me that he just walked in the door.

Eventually the prickly resident comes upstairs from Obstetrics. She examines me and says that the baby's head is crowned. She orders me into a wheelchair so the attendant can take me to the delivery room. On the seemingly endless descent in the elevator, I blow as hard as I can, even though I have the urge to push.

* * *

When my second-born daughter is two months old, Sister Mary Gerald calls once again. As a favor to her, I resume teaching math and science in grades five, six, seven and eight. When I return to school this time, I am the eighth-grade homeroom teacher.

One morning before class a group of inquisitive students gathers at my desk. The chairman of this committee bravely speaks. The consensus is that Mary, the mother of Jesus, had sex with a man and got pregnant nine months before Jesus was born. The pubescent youths unequivocally reject the contrived explanation that Mary's virginity is "a mystery of our faith."

In that moment my students illuminate for me the distinct difference between beliefs that are proliferated from the outside and truths that germinate from center.

* * *

The following year I once again experience abdominal cramps and bleeding atypical of a menstrual cycle. I call my gynecologist to report that I have just suffered another miscarriage. He tells me that because I did not have a confirmed pregnancy, he cannot concur that I actually had a miscarriage.

At 11 o'clock that night, as the doctor performs an emergency DNC, he confirms what I already knew was true. I ask him to show me the evidence of my aborted pregnancy: pieces of placenta removed from my body that now lay in a metal pan in the operating room.

Several months later, when I discover that I am again pregnant, I find a new gynecologist. I approach this pregnancy and delivery with a whole new mindset. With the confidence that I once knew as a young athlete, I now trust my body to do what comes naturally. I decide that when this baby is ready to enter the world, I will rely solely upon my feminine intuitive sense to guide me through the process of labor at home. I will trust completely in my innate maternal instinct.

Before labor begins I devise a plan to inform my husband precisely when we must get into the car and drive to the hospital. In full-blown labor, I mouth the agreed-upon signal, "now," between contractions. I am exasperated when my husband asks, "Are you sure?"

As soon as we arrive at the hospital we are immediately ushered into the delivery room. A labor nurse comments that she has never seen anyone as calm and focused as I am during natural childbirth. Within 15 minutes I contentedly cradle our newborn son in my arms.

* * *

Five years later, as I lie in bed early one morning, I pensively reflect upon my first miscarriage. I feel the ripping internal pain. I feel my body contract and open to release the contents of my uterus. I feel the pressure of the bulging mass as it slips out of my body. Though the fetus is not viable, I am suspended in time as I hold the potential miracle of life and mystery of death in my hands.

At five o'clock sharp, in the moment just before the clock radio is set to awaken us, I hear it click on. The radio announcer begins his morning news broadcast. He talks about an experiment by Doctor T. Berry Brazelton, a well-known pediatrician. (My high school friend who invited me to the luau gave me one of his books on infant care when she was our childbirth instructor.) In this experiment Dr. Brazelton inserted a light into a pregnant woman's uterus. The fetus did not respond. The eyes did not open. The conclusion of the experiment is that the fetus could not see the light.

* * *

I close my eyes and imagine the seed of life I hold in my hands. In my mind I wander through a nebulous space between fertility and infertility. In a passageway that is both light and darkness, I balance in quietude on a delicate precipice between life and death.

Within this journey I see the kaleidoscope of my childhood. I acknowledge that light must enter to awaken the beauty hidden inside the cylinder. Further along the path I come upon the little red berry. Grounded in earth, this seed carries within its nature its path to center, its true home. From my vantage point I embrace this whisper of life infused with air, water and light. I observe its innate ability to emerge from earth and seek out its full potential. I feel my father's love, the active ingredient that nurtured the seed, allowing it to grow and thrive.

On this inward journey I see that life is sustained interiorly, at center. Disconnected from center, life cannot exist. Center is that place where a natural spark enlivens and empowers the seed to release its potential and reach toward the fullness of life.

Angeline

A high school friend – a reserved, dutiful adolescent – is grounded, an innocent victim confined to her bedroom in the basement of her parents' house. In the darkness of night, with a squadron of daring teenaged accomplices, I stealthily slink up the driveway and into the yard. When the awaiting captive pushes open her recessed bedroom window, my enterprising companions and I free her from the underground chamber.

Years later when my family and I live in the two-story house in the town next to my hometown, this reserved friend and her children come to visit. While we adults reminisce over our high-school antics, our older children play outdoors on the swing set in our backyard. Oblivious to our giddiness, the energetic youngsters repeatedly hop off the swings and scamper into the house. They dart back outside with their snacks, bologna roll-ups, which they eat picnic-style on the swing set.

That fall, a week after Thanksgiving, my husband and I go on vacation with our children to Disney World. Late on a Wednesday morning we break for an early lunch at La Cantina De San Angel, a Mexican restaurant in EPCOT, one of the Disney theme parks. Sweltering in the blazing sunshine, I attempt to open the collapsed umbrella that is secured in the center of our outdoor table.

When I reach up inside the folds of the umbrella I feel a horrific pain in my left hand. Bewildered, I see an

Angeline

agitated insect fly out of the still-closed umbrella. With my eyes I follow the culprit's meandering path as it spirals up into the sunlit air. Eyes closed, I visualize the insect's upward journey and focus on this imaginary trail. In that space where I see the kaleidoscope of my childhood, I view the components of an unsolved puzzle, clues to a message that I cannot yet decipher.

Before noon, while my family feasts on tacos and churros, I make the first of two treks to the Disney infirmary. In spite of the medical attention I receive, the excessive swelling and throbbing pain from this curious insect bite persist for several days.

Minutes after arriving home from Florida the following Sunday afternoon, I am surprised when the telephone immediately rings. After my initial hesitation, I answer the phone. The friend who introduced me to my husband in high school politely asks about my family vacation. But, as she speaks, I detect an eerie foreboding in the spaces between her words.

This friend, who was also a member of the daring teenaged squadron in high school, delicately informs me that there was an accident while I was away. Our reserved friend's five-year-old daughter, Angeline, is in the hospital in critical condition.

As I listen to my friend recount the details of the accident, I intuitively ask, "What day did the accident occur?"

She responds, "Wednesday."

Angeline

As I drift to that place of solace deep inside of me where I meet the boy, I hear the fading echo of my next inquiry, "What time...?"

* * *

Gently afloat in my inner sanctuary I imagine myself as a child, the kindergartener who loves being the helper. At my father's meat and grocery store I dust and neatly stock the shelves. With the bottom of a glass jar I crush rock-hard olives and drop them into the homemade brine. I use my thumbs to push freshly ground, seasoned meat through the hollow funnel and into the natural sausage casings. When customers finish shopping I crank the handle on the adding machine to tally up their orders. I open the gilded cash register and place the paper money above the cash drawer before I help my father make change. When I bag groceries I put heavy bottles and cans on the bottom of the brown paper satchel and gently place crushable items on top. At the end of the day I love to scatter fresh-smelling sawdust on the old wooden floor and sweep it clean before my father locks up for the night.

Down the street from my father's store is the north entrance to the Bigelow-Sanford Carpet Mill, the bustling factory where my mother's mother works. Every afternoon when she finishes spinning giant spools of wool on massive, deafening machinery, my grandmother walks to my father's store to buy her groceries. Whenever I'm at the store I always walk back to my grandmother's house with

Angeline

her. I like to help her carry the heavy bundles up the hill and all the way home.

One bright, sunny afternoon I sit on the curb in front of my father's store and wait for my grandmother to get out of work at the mill. I notice my next-door neighbor, Charlie, on the sidewalk behind me leaning against the building next to the store. Playing with the loose stones on the side of the road, I repeatedly pick up small rocks and toss them back down onto the pavement in front of me. Absorbed by this activity, I accidentally throw one stone too far into the street. Without looking up, I automatically slide off the curb and bound into the road to capture the escaping stone.

Now I hear the roaring engine and feel my whole body vibrate with the sound. As the brightness of the afternoon sun disappears I feel like I'm in a dark tunnel. From inside this passageway I see the gigantic wheels of the tractor-trailer truck spin around.

Captured by this distant world I hear Charlie's booming voice echo, "No, no, no…"

When the sunlight reappears I realize that I'm in the middle of the road in front of my father's store. Still lying on the ground, I watch the 18-wheeler slowly make its way up the hill.

* * *

After the phone conversation with the friend who introduced me to my husband in high school, I tearfully tell my husband about Angeline's accident. Nearly every day for the next three weeks I sit and wait in the hallway across from the closed door to Angeline's hospital room. As my reserved friend specifically requests, I do not enter the room.

At the gravesite after Angeline's funeral service I turn to walk back to the car. As I move forward I feel a jolt, an electric charge that prickles my whole body. Instinctively I grasp my left hand with my right, mindful of the incident at La Cantina De San Angel a few weeks earlier. As my hands touch, the crusty scab from the insect bite detaches and falls to the frozen earth. Underneath the old, sloughed scab is healthy, soft, pink tissue that has formed to heal the wound.

Look Up

A curved, 800-foot long driveway leads to our two-story house in the town next to our hometown. The bulk of the acreage stretches out in front of the house while the comparably diminutive backyard borders an expansive field that merges with dense woods. Two weeks after we moved to this rural location, our orange, tiger-striped kitten, Toby, wandered away from home and never returned.

The bush my father grew from a little red berry now thrives in fertile soil near the main entrance to this home. Beyond the front lawn a five-foot, split-rail fence surrounds the generous pastureland and the two-stall barn. The sweet smells of hay in the loft and grain in the feed bin waft through the air. The earthy aroma rising from the oiled leather saddles and bridles in the tack room awakens my senses. I delight in all of the natural, sometimes pungent, odors that flourish in this idyllic setting.

Riding one morning in woodlands a few miles from home, I approach a sign that clearly prohibits trespassers but specifically welcomes horseback riders onto the property. As I energetically trot my horse along the wide, tree-lined trail, I feel a sudden impulse to look up. Silhouetted in bright blue skylight, a large owl, the first I have ever encountered in the wild, regally perches on a lofty tree branch.

Look Up

Destined to look up, I am the child who sees my first kaleidoscope in the space that opens when I close my eyes. Just as light enters the kaleidoscope to illumine the movement of brilliant colors and symmetrical patterns, it now illuminates the beauty and majesty of nature. I revel in the inner stirrings and the sense of dawning that emanate from nature's inspiring displays and rhythms. Here, the world I see with my physical eyes and my inner world are one.

As I ride my horse further along the trail through the woods, I halt at the edge of a clearing dotted with several charming guest cottages. The multi-colored miniature village looks like a whimsical scene from a child's storybook. Through the woods beyond the perfectly manicured guesthouses, I focus on a circular Shaker barn sited near the main residence. From my woodsy perspective on horseback, I now recognize the property that I often pass while driving in my car.

The owner of this striking estate is one of the brothers who founded Friendly Ice Cream. Reportedly, they also owned the shopping mall where the con artist tricked my father with the coin-operated laundry scam when I was in sixth grade.

Despite this abrupt realization, the sights and sounds of nature continue to captivate me. Contented, I turn my horse and canter out of the woods on the same trail on which I entered. One with my horse, I feel the vibration of every hoof beat as it drums on the solid earth. Exhilarated, I hear the whistling air as it meets my body and flows into the beyond.

Look Up

I am at peace in this space where my physical reality and my creative imagination come together. Immersed in nature, I intuitively go to that interior place where I talk with the boy. At center I am liberated from the lingering anguish of keeping my family's secret. At center I am free of the torment of harboring my own guarded inner secret, my concealed interior life.

One night I have a vivid dream that takes place in a crowded cathedral in Hartford. In this colorful vision, a man I know reverently administers Holy Communion to hundreds of awaiting worshippers. When I awaken from this live animation, its powerful images capture my attention and remain actively present in my mind.

A few weeks later the man's wife, the friend who hosted the Hawaiian luau in high school, unexpectedly arrives at a mutual friend's house while I am also there visiting. Motivated by this timely encounter with a friend whom I have not seen for a long time, I deferentially describe the compelling dream I had about her husband.

Astonished, she informs me that her husband, the boy who pushed me down at the big house when I was a child, was recently ordained as a Eucharistic minister. As her words flow through me, I instantly enter that space where my physical reality and my creative imagination are one. As I inwardly look up, I intuitively envision the cathedral in my dream, the precise location of the actual ceremony.

A Second Chance

An informal dinner party with close friends ends abruptly when one person angrily explodes, "You owe me money!" On the car ride home I am deeply troubled by this unexpected remark. That night sleep evades me as the verbal barrage echoes in my mind and induces a disturbing undercurrent.

In a discussion with the irate man's wife the next day, I learn that she and her husband contend that my husband bought theater tickets at a discount and then charged the couple full price. This inane allegation astounds me, but the unwarranted distrust of dear friends devastates me. In a desperate attempt to restore harmony and patch a once-valued friendship, I trustingly confide in this friend and explain how false accusations have previously ravaged me.

Days after I attempt to repair our relationship, the woman calls to ask why I have not responded to her invitation to their son's upcoming christening. When I tell her that I did not receive an invitation she promises to send another. Before the invitation arrives she calls a second time to pointedly ask why I have not responded. When I truthfully tell her that I have not yet received the invitation in the mail, she retorts that "someone" at my house saw the invitation on my refrigerator.

Stunned by this brazen remark, I assure her that I did not receive her christening invitation. I then clarify that the invitation displayed on my refrigerator is to a baby shower for my husband's cousin.

A Second Chance

Overtly accused of lying, I once again succumb to the indescribable anguish generated by false accusations, betrayal by people in whom I've placed my unwavering love and trust. I relive the sorrow of my father's victimizations and the torment of my mother's deception.

In the safety of my inner sanctuary, I review events in my life as if I am watching a play on a theater stage. I meticulously analyze specific scenes and scrutinize explicit conversations. As a narrative of my whole life crystallizes I notice that repetitive patterns and parallels emerge. Cocooned in my interior refuge, I freely articulate all of my unexpressed feelings to the only one who understands me, certain that one day I will reunite with the boy.

In an effort to diligently conceal my fragile interior state, I intentionally bury myself in the mounting responsibilities of home, family and church community. I robotically subsist, secretly yearning to escape from the stress of my frenzied existence. In my imagination, I fearlessly wander beyond the garden in the side yard at the big house of my childhood. Confident, I intermingle with the forbidden gypsies adorned in brightly colored costumes. Infused with an optimistic, adventuresome spirit, I follow a luminous pathway to center, my true home, and revitalize my exuberance for life.

Several months later I gently inform my mother that my husband plans to accept the promising position in Boston that I had recently discussed with her at length. Upon receiving this update she counters, "How can you do this to me?" Fixed on the panoramic view outside her cozy in-law apartment she glumly adds, "How can you leave everything you love so much and worked so hard to get?"

After an exhaustive, unproductive discussion, I ask my mother why she always supports my sister but never supports me in any major decisions that I make. She immediately laments, "Because she's weak and needs me, but you're strong and you don't need me."

Dazed by this response, I am speechless when she audibly mutters, "I never should have had a second child."

My sister, in camaraderie with our mother, severs her association with me. She shuns me when she visits our mother at my house. She neither speaks to me nor acknowledges my existence.

Disheartened, I acquiesce to my debilitating sadness and seek counsel from a priest at my church. At our single meeting in the parish rectory I disclose the heartache triggered by false accusations leveled by people I love and trust. I describe the revived anguish over my mother's threat to withhold forgiveness if I ever reveal the secret that she and my sister keep. I explain the resurrected grief over my inability to be truthful with my now-deceased father.

At a pregnant pause in this personal account, the cleric abruptly rises from his chair and strides to the door. With one hand on the doorknob he turns to me and comments, "And we come from the good families. Imagine what it's like for people who come from bad families."

A Second Chance

During the summer, while I search for a new home near Boston and prepare my family for the transition, I remain active on several church committees. One day I place a phone call to a woman who serves with me in the church community. After I identify myself to the man who answers the phone, he repeats my name and muses, "Now that's a name I haven't heard in a long time."

Now living in New Orleans, the artist is visiting with his sister and her family in our hometown. Struggling to contain my exhilaration, I spontaneously invite him to spend an afternoon at my home.

Sitting in my backyard by the outdoor pool we watch my children splash in the crystal-clear water. As we connect, seemingly by chance, for only the second time since high school, tender memories of carefree summer days with our tightly knit group of teen-aged friends swim in my mind. As we easily converse, with gently flowing words he paints an alluring portrait of divine love and spiritual fulfillment. Buoyant in an ocean that has no water, I am filled with a powerful presence, a burning love that ignites from within and wholly envelops me. In my creative imagination I am a transparent body of water through which he sees the real me, at center, in that interior space that is home to Truth.

The thoughts swirling in my mind rapidly transform into vivid depictions of dreams and inward conversations with the boy that I long to share aloud. Free to communicate intimately with him in my interior refuge, I now squander my second chance to confide in the man who sits before me. Constrained by fear and self-imposed doubt, I safeguard my inner secret and remain voiceless.

Disillusioned by my own inadequacy, I retreat to my inner sanctuary where I instantaneously view a luminous scene from my childhood. Always the helper, I attentively watch my father empty the weighty water from the holding tank of the heavy lawn roller to make my job manageable. Observing this instructive event, I intuitively know that one day I will overcome my own limitations. Once liberated, I will find my voice and realize the work that lies ahead.

In mid-August I drive to Boston to meet my husband at the hotel where he is temporarily living. When I open my luggage I discover that by mistake I have hastily grabbed my children's identical suitcase packed with their clothing instead of mine. After dinner that night, our dear friends whisk us to the Chestnut Hill Mall to buy all the essentials, including a complete outfit for me to wear to the closing at our attorney's office the next day.

* * *

One week before our move to the Boston suburbs, our family mourns the death of our dog, Teddy, the feisty, black puppy with brown markings that I had brought home from school nine years before.

* * *

A Second Chance

On Labor Day weekend I make a last visual sweep of our empty, two-story house in the town next to our hometown. Ready to take our teen-aged babysitter home, we pile into the overloaded station wagon, drive down the long, curved driveway and proceed to her nearby house.

As we pull into her driveway for the last time, a distinctively marked cat saunters across the generous front yard and ambles across the street. Probingly I ask, "Whose cat is that?"

The young lady explains that the cat, a stray, doesn't belong to anyone. She and her neighbor take turns feeding the independent, orange, tiger-striped feline who wandered into her yard as a kitten seven years ago.

This timely revelation that Toby is alive rekindles an ember planted deeply inside of me. Although blanketed in sadness, I realize that the resurgence of our lost kitten, now grown, is a glorious symbol of undying *hope*.

As I embark on my journey, I spiral back to my childhood and hear the echo of my father's guidance that I must be patient and wait to see what happens to the little red berry concealed beneath the soil. This recollection affirms my inner knowing, a strong conviction that I must wait for a sign, an incontrovertible revelation, offering me the optimum moment to unearth the buried secret of my interior world.

A Sculpture in the Garden

Two weeks after the closing I'm eager to settle my family into the multi-level residence in a suburb of Boston. When we arrive at our new address I am flabbergasted to find the previous owner still living in our house. Relegated to staying at a Sheraton Hotel for the next three days, my husband and I minimize the seriousness of our dilemma and cheerfully announce to our children that we have a surprise. We are going on a mini vacation where they will have fun swimming in a heated indoor pool.

Before dawn on the first morning that I awaken in our new home, I quietly descend the stairs and meander into the kitchen. Initially deeming the entire house livable in its existing condition, I now survey the room that will be the center of our family gatherings. I visually note the drab green carpeting, the murky brown cabinets, the mud-colored wainscoting, the dated copper-toned appliances, the puny window and the two closed interior doors that isolate the kitchen from the rest of the house.

Caged in this dungeon, I impulsively grasp a corner of the dingy carpet and try to rip it from the underlying linoleum squares. I discover that the carpet is securely glued to the floor and must apply an all-purpose hammer to pry the rug from the hardened adhesive. Occupied with my early morning task, I futilely explain to my now-awake husband that I must open the blocked space to allow the natural light to enter. Incredulous, he mutters some indiscernible sounds and turns to amble back up the stairway.

The next month I accompany my husband on a business trip to historic New Orleans, the city where the artist now resides. Meeting with him for the third time since high school, he talks about his spiritual path as we stroll along the sun-drenched sidewalk. Absorbed in conversation, I suddenly feel lightheaded and dizzy. My internal exhilaration spontaneously burgeons into a compelling, radiant energy that simultaneously envelops and incapacitates me.

My eyes look up toward a vibrantly colored flower garden that draws me in close. Called to this oasis, I ascend the stairs that lead to the side entrance of the hotel where I may reach the garden. Drained, I collapse in the garden on a cement wall that encircles a refreshing pool of sparkling water.

As I regain my strength and look up into the natural sunlight, an alluring sculpture captures my attention and transfixes me with ecstasy. I feel increasingly fortified as I gaze at the tall, slim figure that beckons me to bask in its glorious presence.

The next morning while talking on the phone with the artist, he asks if I know the name of the sculpture that captivated me. When I answer "no," he tells me that the piece is entitled "Godman."

Rapt by this revelation, I instinctively share with the artist that I understand his special gift of inner perception. I then tell him that he has the potential to be a powerful spiritual influence in this lifetime.

A Sculpture in the Garden

As I drift into the space that opens when I close my eyes, I distance myself from the fading echo of the artist's ethereal response, "It's not me. It's you…"

* * *

Afloat in my interior sanctuary I intuitively recall a repressed memory from my childhood. I want to run and hide but I cannot escape from the disturbing voice inside of me. I am frightened and ashamed to inwardly hear the strange message, "One day you will be famous. People will know who you are."

* * *

The following is an excerpt from my first journal entry penned on the flight home from New Orleans in October 1984:

The Holy Spirit moves among us in ways I don't always understand. Sometimes it's frightening.

Sometimes I want to deny thoughts and feelings, to feel safe and secure by not being aware of them, but I must accept what is to be, not question it.

Sometimes I'm scared because I don't know where I'm going, but not so scared that I want this journey to end.

Sometimes it's difficult not fitting in anywhere, but comforting to be contented with my own presence.

There's always more to know, more to understand. But I learned long ago that I'm not living this life for me. Somehow I feel that there is a larger purpose in store for me, though I don't know what it is.

Out of Stillness

At Catskill Game Farm in upstate New York I nestle my fingers into a lamb's curly fleece and stroke a baby goat's flat coat. The frisky animals in the children's petting zoo cluster around me to munch on the crackers I offer them and guzzle from the milk bottle I hold in my hands. When the largest among my four-footed friends get too rambunctious, I fling some tasty treats for all of them to chase. When they run to the food, they naturally open a space for the smaller mammals to snuggle close to me.

While I play near the picnic tables I notice a large outcrop in the distance. Curious, I wander away from my family to investigate. When I realize that the rock is actually a statue of a camel, I race across the grassy field, eager to go on an imaginary ride. I lift my left foot way up high and step into a hole on the camel's side. I swing my right leg up and over the hump to mount the pretend steed.

At the end of my make-believe escapade, I slide my left foot into the same opening and swing my right leg over to dismount. Clinging to the statue, I look in both directions to see if anyone notices that I am stuck. No matter how hard I try, I can't pull my foot out of the hole. While I silently wait for someone to help me get unstuck, I look up into the sunlit sky.

Suddenly I feel two strong hands grasp me by the waist and lift me up into the air, allowing me to dislodge my jammed foot and set myself free.

Out of Stillness

* * *

Now living in our home in a Boston suburb, I spend many winter weekends skiing with my family in New Hampshire's White Mountains. While I meander down the snow-packed slopes, I pay particular attention to the open sky and the breathtaking panoramic views. Wrapped in nature, I feel distanced from the invisible gloom that lurks inside my body.

Evocative memories inevitably return as I relive certain scenes from my past. As I vividly recollect walking with the artist in New Orleans, my mind replays every word of our conversation. Even though months have lapsed, I continue to scrutinize each detail of our stroll along the city sidewalk. I contemplate my deep feelings and the burning desire that drew me in close to the flower garden, the refreshing water and the "Godman" sculpture.

Springtime arrives and the earth reawakens but I remain buried in my own darkness. I wonder if the unconventional events in my life are real. In addition to reliving the pain of past betrayals and false accusations, I now resurrect other haunting memories that greatly distress me.

In my mind I hear a friend sing "Cherish," her favorite song in high school. Several years later, this innocent newlywed was abducted during a bank robbery and murdered. Next I see the dusty, insect-covered body of a young woman with long braids lying face up on the shoulder of a well-traveled road. Dozens of motorists had driven passed this unconscious victim but no one had stopped to help her. Then I picture my former neighbor, the husband of the math teacher in junior high school, on the day he unexpectedly came to visit at my house. After playing with my daughters and cradling my infant son in his arms, he returned home to end his life.

Standing motionless in the shower one morning I feel every pulsating drop of water pelt my weary body. I long for the purifying liquid to wash away my hopelessness. I look up at the silvery fountainhead, the source of the potent flow, and gently close my eyes. Out of stillness a distinct voice commands, *Trust in God and no one else.*

Trust Me

Trust in God and no one else. I wonder if this is the long-awaited sign, the revelation, to guide me toward the optimum moment to reveal my guarded inner secret. But now that the time may have come, I hesitate...

* * *

Dripping wet, I turn off the steamy flow of water, open the fogged-up glass door and blurt, "Who's there?"

I wrap my body in a blue terrycloth towel and step out of the shower enclosure. A draft of rushing air braces me as I open the bathroom door. I walk out of the master bedroom and stand on the second floor landing. Peering down the stairs into the vacant front foyer I wonder aloud, "Is anyone here?"

In profound stillness I solemnly reverse my direction, retrace my footsteps and return to the shower stall. The pulsating spray from the silvery fountainhead resumes its rhythmic beat and pummels my drained body. In the space that opens when I close my eyes I sense a powerful invisible presence.

Simultaneously I feel a riveting spark ignite deep inside of me. At center, this gleaming flame immediately explodes into a rampant fire. The searing energy envelops my entire being and obliterates all boundaries between it and me. Awestruck, I dissolve into the luminosity of this glorious radiance.

Trust Me

This ethereal phenomenon spontaneously transforms into a driving force, a powerful interior directive that compels me to take action. As if decoding cryptic instructions, I intuitively know what I must do to answer this divine call.

For several days my mind grapples with inner turmoil and struggles with the complex challenge of facing my true self. *Do I have the right to impose upon him? Is revealing my truth in his best interest? Will he think I'm crazy?*

In a bold effort to dispel my trepidation I nervously clutch the phone. When he answers, the words I mentally rehearsed in preparation for this imminent conversation are lost to insecurity and self-doubt. Wavering, I recollect our last conversation in New Orleans when he mysteriously said, "It's not me. It's you…" before informing him that I have something important to discuss with him, a spiritual matter that is of value to both of us.

Intuitively, I know that the artist is silently considering my request to speak with him in person. Hopeful, I remind myself that I am not alone on this endless quest for truth and meaning in life. Afloat in a sea of stillness, I hear my father's faint echo: *Wait and see what happens…*

But at this pivotal juncture of potential transformation I am pregnant with gestating truth and obscured consequence. Burning with a fervent desire to liberate my true self, I unexpectedly hear my own voice break the silence.

Trust me…

Trust Me

* * *

In the bustling terminal at Logan Airport, with my husband at my side, I anxiously watch every passenger emerge from the jetway. The artist is not among the dwindling stream of travelers who walk toward me. Disillusioned, I remain frozen in place for several minutes. Suddenly I turn my attention to the voices coming from the enclosed passageway. An attractive flight attendant exits the jetway and walks into the terminal. Strolling nonchalantly beside her is a single straggler, the very last passenger to disembark the aircraft.

That evening, in the safety of my home, I initiate the intricate exchange that I have deftly avoided for 20 years. Guided by spirit, I confide in the artist and launch into the story of my life. As I listen, I hear my own voice recount the same inner conversations that I previously shared with the boy in my interior sanctuary, in the space that opens when I close my eyes.

But now I speak with my eyes open. I hear my voice sing and I feel my body dance. Familiar with the verses and the steps, I meander through the twists and turns of my life. As past and present meet in the here and now, I am living testament to the existence of an awakened state in which the inner and the outer, the spiritual and the physical, are One.

The Next Step

Sitting on the pale-green carpet in my living room, I inhale deeply, poised to embark upon the pivotal next step in my life's journey, hopeful that this intimate passage will liberate me from the debilitating grip of depression.

During my confidential exchange with the artist, I listen to my own voice release each carefully phrased sentence. The precise words that I use to divulge my innermost secrets emanate from that sacred interior space where only truth resides. As the free-flowing narrative unfolds, enduring memories emerge as specific visions in my mind. Inwardly I see my beloved kindergarten teacher, Sister Mary Amelda, whose incisive recognition cultivated my innate yearning to be "the helper."

With sure trust I confide in the artist just as I share my truth with "the boy" in the safety of my inner sanctuary. I freely articulate all of my unexpressed feelings to the only one who I believe understands me. As I listen to my own voice tell the story, I recognize the repetitive patterns and parallels that emerge within the twists and turns of the unfolding plot.

I meticulously unearth the long-lived secrets that silenced my voice. I acknowledge the sorrow of my father's victimizations and the torment of my mother's deception. I describe how false accusations triggered the major depressions that have challenged my life. I examine my vulnerability in attempting to befriend people who

The Next Step

dismiss inner truth, harbor old grudges and firmly cling to their opinions. This methodical exercise in analysis and synthesis reveals why I tend to disengage from those who have not learned to open their hearts and forgive.

In the chronicle of my life story I journey back to the historical city of New Orleans. When I inwardly re-enter the vibrant flower garden and encounter the awe-inspiring sculpture, "Godman," I respond equally as intensely as I did when the artist first told me its name.

I now repeat the words I said to the artist on that auspicious morning. Once again I tell him that I resonate with his gift of inner perception and that I believe he has the potential to be a powerful spiritual influence in this lifetime.

As if on cue, he resolutely holds my gaze and pointedly reiterates, *It's not me. It's you...*

In utter disbelief I again refute this preposterous assumption and firmly maintain that I'm just a girl from Thompsonville, insignificant and unworthy of special consideration. I insist that he, the boy from my hometown, is the one blessed with a capacity for spiritual distinction.

Despite my resolve the artist persists in his claim that the spiritual acuity of which we speak lives within me. He assures me that until now, he was unaware of my feelings for him and my interior connection with "the boy." He tells me that my body is my connection to the divine and that my burning desire within is the love of God.

The Next Step

As I try to listen intently to what he says I instead hear only a muffled drone as if he is talking to me in slow motion. My mind cannot grasp the enormity of what he professes to be true. Reeling, my thoughts gravitate to the words that came in the shower that memorable hopeless morning, the words that impelled me to invite him to my home.

I tentatively ask the artist whose voice he thinks I heard command, *Trust in God and no one else.*

Aflame in an ocean with no water, I dissolve into the muted echo of his astonishing response, *It's you. It's your voice…*

* * *

In the ensuing interlude I visually witness a transformation in the artist's physical appearance. As his facial features blur and elongate, his ears become pointy and extend upward on both sides of his head. Intrigued but not frightened, I automatically exude boundless compassion and silently counter this curious aberration with an intense outpouring of infinite unconditional love. When the graphic distortion gradually reverts back to its familiar form I simply resume my dialogue with the artist.

Convinced that I must fully disclose every aspect of my life story, I share an enigmatic prophecy that I have heard inwardly: one day I will reveal my truth to the world. I tell him that I have been guided to wait for a sign, a revelation that will guide my next step.

The Next Step

The next morning I open the new books that the artist has brought with him on this visit to our home, books that until now, I would have intentionally avoided. In perusing these texts I realize that other seekers have had mysterious experiences that resonate with mine. Filled with gratitude, I hold in my hands the first tangible evidence that validates the integrity of my interior existence. Like a reverberating echo of my former eighth grade students, the writers of these passages illuminate the distinct difference between beliefs that are proliferated from the outside and truths that germinate from within, from the center of our being.

Maneuvering through this ongoing process of self-discovery and healing, I feel the immobilizing grip of depression lighten its hold on me. However, the migraine headaches that I have suffered for seven years become increasingly worse and frequently incapacitate me. During this transitional shift in awareness I practice relaxation and visualization techniques and wholeheartedly focus on my spiritual growth and development.

Just as I once listened to the whir of a helicopter when I was a child, I now place my awareness on the humming that emanates from within. I notice that sometimes I feel disconnected and cannot hear this interior sound. I experiment and learn that I can call this inner vibration back to me by gently shifting my consciousness. I come to realize that this high-pitched resonance is always present, but that I cannot hear it when my attention wanders away from center.

The Next Step

Throughout this time of spiritual exploration and transformation I remain faithful to my religion and actively participate in my new church community. While talking with the musical director after church one Sunday morning I learn that she is a professional piano teacher. With piqued interest I ask her to accept me as one of her students. At my first piano lesson she discovers that in my college courses on music theory I had acquired the technical ability to transpose sheet music into various scales, but that I never learned how to play an instrument.

During my second lesson the musical director asks me to join the church choir. I tell her that I cannot sing very well and respectfully decline her offer. She invites me to sit with the choir at their next performance. At church that Sunday I walk up to the balcony where my piano teacher waits for me. She hands me a pile of sheet music and asks me to sit between two talented singers, one a soprano and the other an alto.

The inspiring music awakens my senses and touches my heart. The harmonious notes from the two distinct melodic ranges simultaneously carry me away and draw me in close. Sometimes I find myself singing in unison with the lower register, sometimes merging into the higher realm. My voice follows the notes as if they are stepping-stones on a path to the center of my self.

On Our Way Home

One afternoon our sixteen-year-old babysitter, a neighbor, calls unexpectedly to say that if I need her help, she is available to watch my three children. When she arrives I rush to the barn and saddle up my chestnut mare for an impromptu jaunt through the woods. Trotting along interconnected trails that I've yet to explore, I feel a blustery chill in the air as the sun rapidly descends in the winter sky.

As I wind my way back to the barn, Frolic nervously hesitates at a fork in the road. When we reach the end of the branched trail that I've chosen to follow, I realize I've taken a wrong turn. When I reverse direction my mare hastens her pace as daylight quickly fades to dusk. When we come to another divide in the trail, I am acutely aware of Frolic's heightened anxiety and immediately loosen my hold on the braided leather reins, allowing her to lead me out of the darkness.

* * *

Lounging on the couch in my living room, my thoughts drift to meeting the boy on the last day of school in eighth grade and reconnecting with him at the Hawaiian luau the following year. Merging with the reverberant inner whirring, I soar in everlasting memories of the special friendship that blossomed during that summer of innocence. I acknowledge the heartache I felt when we parted ways and the fervor of my conviction that I would one day reunite with the boy. I rekindle the urgency of my relentless search for him and marvel at our seemingly chance encounters. Rapt, I am One with the resounding directive, *Trust in God and no one else*, that compelled me to break my silence and unearth my guarded inner secret.

On this luminous voyage through profound stillness, nebulous fragments of my life assimilate into a cohesive whole. This ongoing process of synthesis fuels a fountainhead of self-awareness and intuitive knowing. Ablaze, I fuse with a dazzling silhouette of my inner secret, a radiant truth that I've long concealed from myself. Sheltered in this fiery enclave I clearly see that my unrelenting search for the boy is a guise for my endless quest to align with my true self.

From the center of my being, a burning desire, fed by the source of my aliveness, embodies my love of God. This insatiable yearning illumines the certainty that my body is my inner sanctuary, my link to the divine. Here, at center, I intuitively know that my interior communication with "the boy" is an echo of my own voice, my own truth that emanates from the depths of my being.

But fear and self-doubt inevitably enter my mind, erode my confidence and prompt unfathomable questions. *Is all of this real? Why is this happening to me? What am I here to do? Is anyone here to help me?*

Overwhelmed, I swirl in the intoxicating energy that abundantly streams from the Source deep inside of me.

On Our Way Home

Attempting to balance this illumined existence with my everyday life, I remind myself that I'm undeserving of divine favors.

As I quiet my mind and return to stillness, I relive the moment when I allowed my horse to lead me out of the darkness on our way back home. In my vision I focus on the subtle movement of my hands as I release my hold on the braided reins and give Frolic her head. I clearly see that when I trust myself enough to relinquish control and rely upon my mare's natural instinct, I enhance my innate connection to an existence beyond myself. I expand my freedom to simply be and activate my essential craving for inner exploration and spiritual adventure.

* * *

On a spring field trip with my older daughter and her fourth-grade class, I climb the broad steps, walk through a massive double door and enter the historic Boston Public Library. Our female guide leads us down the hallway and outdoors to an open-air courtyard. As I walk along the herringbone-patterned red brick path, my body feels inexplicably charged with energy. Bemused, I focus my attention on the center of the garden, an enclosed quadrangle that mysteriously captivates me.

At the end of the walkway we re-enter the building and file into the Microtext Department where printed archives are stored. A double row of two-dozen microfiche readers runs lengthwise down the middle of the narrow room and divides the space into two long, parallel aisles. The students listen attentively as an experienced librarian explains the proper use of the machines and demonstrates how to thread and advance the film to view historical documents.

At the end of the session the fourth-grade teacher asks the class to line up at the door. From the back of the room I see my daughter hesitantly inch her way toward the exit. As I approach her, she abruptly turns around and rushes past me. When I tell her that it's time to go she anxiously blurts, "Mom, I can't leave. There's something here I have to find."

In a room brimming with microfiche readers I quietly observe as my fourth-grader races to a random machine, sits down on a boxy wooden chair and advances the microfiche in fast forward motion. I hear a distinct mechanical chatter as the film glides under the glass plate and winds around the take-up reel. Mesmerized, I silently stand beside my daughter and watch as an amorphous blur speeds across the face of the monitor.

At a precise moment she spontaneously releases the control that advances the film. The rattling microfiche reader abruptly stops. My daughter instinctively points to the bottom right-hand corner of the screen as she looks up at me and says, "This is it. This is meant for me."

My eyes focus on the exact spot where my nine-year-old confidently points with her index finger. Amazed, I hastily jot down the title of the article and the archival information that appears at the top of the monitor. It reads: "Greatness of Soul."

* * *

Fifteen years later I return to the Boston Public Library. As I follow the red brick path through the open-air courtyard I once again feel an electrifying energy pulsate throughout my body. A statue set in the center of a fountain in the inviting garden draws me in close and piques my curiosity, but I resist my natural inquisitiveness. Eager to accomplish my mission, I single-mindedly proceed to the Microtext room. Feeling rejuvenated without knowing why, I advance the selected film in the microfiche reader and locate the specific document that my daughter found when she was in fourth grade.

In celebration of her twenty-fifth birthday, I give her a photocopy of the following article that was published in *The Massachusetts Centinel* on Saturday, July 4, 1789, 13 years after the signing of the Declaration of Independence, aware of the significance that it holds for me.

Greatness of Soul

An anecdote, in "A Tour of Corsica," will illustrate the position, that true greatness of soul may be found as well in the lower as in the highest grades of life. – The leader of a gang of banditti, who had long been famous for his exploits, was at length taken and committed to the care of a soldier, from whom he contrived to escape. The soldier was tried, and condemned to death. At the place of execution, a man, coming up to the commanding officer, says, "Sir, I am a stranger to you, but you shall soon know who I am. I have heard one of your soldiers is to die for having suffered a prisoner to escape: He was not at all to blame; besides, the prisoner shall be restored to you. Behold him here: I am the man. I cannot bear that innocent man should be punished for me, and I come to die myself." – *"No," cried the French officer, who felt the sublimity of the action as he ought, "thou shalt not die, and the soldier shall be set at liberty. Endeavor to reap the fruits of thy generosity: Thou deservest to be henceforth an honest man."*

* * *

Twenty-two years after her fourth grade field trip to the Boston Public Library, my daughter, divorced after suffering a betrayal in her first marriage, reconnects with a classmate with whom she'd lost touch after high school. Now her husband and the father of their infant daughter, he was born on July 4, 1976, the celebrated bicentennial (200th anniversary) of the United States of America.

In the history of this country, two signers of the Declaration of Independence rose to the office of the presidency. Both esteemed men, John Adams and Thomas Jefferson died on July 4, 1826, on the fiftieth anniversary of the birth of freedom for this nation.

Currently, scholarly dissertations on the lives of these two influential figures continue to stimulate debate regarding the existence of parallels between their ideals and the principles of Freemasonry.

* * *

As I record these unique events in my life, the compelling energy that twice captivated me in the courtyard at the Boston Public Library surges through my body and enlivens me. I call the library and speak with a Fine Arts reference librarian to inquire about the mystifying statue in their courtyard.

I learn that the sculpture is a replica of the bronze original, *Bacchante and Infant Faun*, created by Frederick William MacMonnies in 1893. The life-size nude female figure holds a bunch of grapes in one hand and an infant in the other. Viewed by modern art critics as a depiction of the joy of life and the vitality of a mother playing with her child, in 1897 an earlier model was deemed controversial.

In 1993, 100 years after the original was sculpted, a new *Bacchante* was cast in bronze and delivered to the Boston Public Library. In triumph over her misconstrued meaning as a symbol of indecency and frivolity, she was re-installed in the center of the garden in 2000.

I realize that in 1987, on my daughter's fourth-grade class trip to the Boston Public Library, the statue wasn't there; the space was empty. Remembering the energy that surged through me that day long ago, when I entered the empty courtyard, the garden echoes the interior space that opens when I close my eyes.

I look up the definition of "bacchante": a priestess or female votary of Bacchus, the god of wine and intoxication. I explore further and learn that a female votary is a woman who takes a vow to dedicate her life to religious worship or service, a woman who devotes herself to a religion or a cause.

As I contemplate the significance of the *Bacchante* and resonate with the concept of a female votary, the whirring sound inside of me rises to a riotous decibel. I re-enter the vibrantly colored flower garden in New Orleans where the alluring sculpture, "Godman," captures my attention and transfixes me with ecstasy. Threading to the past, illumined in brilliance, the gardener at Barbara Dean's in Ogunquit lovingly cultivates various flowers, hearty bushes and sturdy trees. From his shirt pocket he removes a prayer card with a picture of a colorful garden. He kindly hands it to me, newly wed, and gently assures me that God will always be with me.

* * *

In perpetual transformation, I am witness to my own existence. Firmly rooted in earth, I am the little red berry, graced by unconditional love. Burgeoning with potential energy and a dynamic life force, I carry within my nature my own unique, indelible path to center, my true home.

A New Path

Our next-door neighbors, both physicians, live in a contemporary home at the end of a long driveway that borders our property. When they elatedly expect their third child, our families assemble on the screened porch at our house in the Boston suburbs to communally select a name for their baby. In subsequent years we twice reconvene on this porch to choose fitting names for their dogs, Murphy Brown, a chocolate Labrador Retriever, and India Ink, a Scottish Terrier. Our children, often inseparable, combine our last names and affectionately dub our collective family circle the "Krusdy's."

My longtime running partner, Margot, and I frequently welcome the dawn in the midst of our early morning jaunts. Exceedingly responsible in our everyday lives, we thrive upon our joyous belly laughter when we are together. Self-proclaimed life-long students, we relish novel experiences and delight in our joint escapades. These include imaginative practical jokes, experiments in the kitchen with untested recipes and clandestine inspections of new houses that are under construction.

A distinguished hematologist, esteemed Harvard Medical School professor and published author, Margot and I share an active interest in solving puzzles and playing word games. We both savor the creative aspects of language and often discuss the nature of our writings,

A New Path

even though our personal styles and objectives are unique to our callings.

Deep in conversation one morning, on the last leg of a seven-mile jog, Margot proposes that one day I will write a book.

* * *

After vacationing on the Cape for 20 years, my husband and I begin our search for a summer home in a quaint village of Barnstable where neighbors in the Boston suburbs own a beach house. In the fall we meet with a real estate agent, a former teacher, who immediately bonds with our family. She shows us a few houses for sale but none of the properties appeal to us.

Speaking confidentially, the real estate agent informs us that she has the perfect house for us, but it's not yet on the market. The vintage 1896 residence, formerly owned by her husband's now-deceased parents, is held in the Twitchell estate and must go through probate court. Certain that this is the house for us, she asks if we can be patient and wait until the spring.

From our limited vantage point inside our parked car we briefly assess our prospective house on Main Street: the exterior shingles are worn thin, the trim paint is peeling and the green wooden shutters are decrepit. Rickety steps fall away from the partially crumbling foundation, and a bent water pipe serves as a makeshift handrail. The dilapidated stockade fence on the side of the property is rotting on the ground and the barn in the backyard is collapsing.

* * *

Early spring, shortly after my daughter's eventful class trip to the Boston Public Library, I return to the Cape with my family and tour the inside of the antique beach house for the first time. Mismatched cabinets with assorted hardware hang on the cracked kitchen walls. Clumps of loose plaster freely fall from the dining room ceiling. Sheets of bespattered vinyl flooring and oddly shaped pieces of wood are glued onto the tub in the upstairs bathroom. The electrical wiring is knob and tube and the inefficient furnace looks like a monstrous octopus that occupies half the basement.

In May, on our son's fifth birthday, we become the third owners of this turn-of-the-century, shingle-style dwelling that is graced with a flared gambrel roof. As we gradually sort the contents of our new vacation home we discover several hidden treasures: long-concealed pocket doors between the dining room and the living room, wainscoting behind the Formica-covered walls, a maple floor underneath the kitchen linoleum, claw feet on the now-exposed cast-iron bathtub, detailed woodworking under thick layers of paint on the front door and, buried in a heap of broken windows in the basement, the original French doors for the parlor entry.

A New Path

Rummaging through a scrap pile in the basement, I find an angular metal object with the letter "G" in the center. Our children playfully imagine that the "G" stands for our last name, Gowdy, so I place the unique discovery in a visible location on a windowsill on our screened porch, the sign's venerated home for the next 12 years.

* * *

Twenty-two years after finding this metal sign, I will discover the connection between this symbol and the sacred geometry that sometimes forms the basis of a labyrinth's pattern.

* * *

Comfortably nestled in the warm sand on Loop Beach for the first time this summer, I meditate upon the ocean's sparkling dance as its undulating surface reflects the dazzling sunlight. On the horizon the ferryboats appear minuscule as they transport passengers to and from Nantucket and Martha's Vineyard. In my immediate vista, sailboats tack in zigzag to maneuver through the channel between Sampson's Island and the mainland. On their way into the harbor, motorboats cut their speed to reduce the roar of their engines to a muffled drone.

Fully absorbed, I suddenly rouse from my contemplative tranquility when I hear an enthusiastic voice curiously ask, "What are *you* doing here?"

A New Path

Shading my eyes from the brilliant sunshine, I look up and recognize the mother of two little girls who formerly attended nursery school with my two younger children. Reunited for the first time since she moved to Boston's Beacon Hill, I learn that she owns a summer home in the village near mine.

Delighted to rekindle our friendship, I gratefully accept her spontaneous invitation to attend a Fourth of July clambake, a celebration that launches an annual tradition that we maintain for 19 years.

* * *

As soon as we move into our antique beach house, I begin the early morning practice of jogging for an hour before I play tennis. At the break of dawn on a clear mid-summer day, I feel especially energized and decide to run a few extra miles. Nearly home, I see a man in his sixties walk out of the Kettle Ho, the local restaurant. Wearing shorts and carrying a newspaper, he crosses School Street and waits for me to jog passed him on the sidewalk before he steps up onto the curb. I cheerfully thank him and he replies, "Good morning." Smiling back at him, I respond likewise.

In a few strides, as I turn the corner at the gas station on Main and School Streets, a mighty voice radiates from every direction and breaks through the heavenly blue sky.

Your patience is rewarded.

I abruptly stop. Keenly aware of my surroundings I notice that the townspeople walk about and chat as usual; motorists drive their cars down the street as if nothing unusual has happened. Fascinated, I realize that this extraordinary event is not a public declaration but a private revelation, as was the directive, *Trust in God and no one else*. As I ponder the mystery of twice hearing an ethereal voice, I propel my body forward and jog along the uneven sidewalk on my way back home.

Sidetracked from playing tennis, I decide to make a special breakfast for my soon-to-awaken children. While I stand at the kitchen stove and flip pancakes on the griddle, Margot drops by for an impromptu visit. She asks if I jogged on the private road along the ocean. When I answer "no," she exclaims, "I knew it! I knew you would obey those Private Road signs. Those signs are meant for motor vehicles, not for us. You missed a wonderful opportunity. We'll go together."

Aware of this morning's mystical event, my friend's inviting words underscore its message: *Your patience is rewarded*. I am called to courage, to expand beyond the rules, beyond my fear and self-doubt, to delve into the depths of my being, to unlock my truth and to experience the fullness of life.

* * *

Later that morning I contact the artist, the only person I trust with such information. He is on a working vacation, painting on the Cape. At the end of our lengthy conversation, he asks if I would pick him up in

A New Path

Provincetown when his workshop ends in a couple of weeks and drive him to Logan Airport.

At home in the Boston suburbs on the night before this expedition, I fall asleep listening to the pounding rain. I abruptly wake up at four o'clock in the morning with a clear inner knowing: I must bring my car to the artist by 8 a.m. because he has something to do, but he doesn't want to walk in the rain.

Trusting myself, I jump out of bed, quickly get dressed and drive for three hours in a heavy downpour. When I arrive at the art studio three hours ahead of the appointed time, the artist greets me at the door and says, "You're early. But as long as you're here, can I borrow your car? There's something I have to do."

* * *

In the car on the way to the airport, the ease of our conversation is a swift current that carries me back to our poolside dialogue when we connected for the second time since high school. The artist's gentle words assemble into a brilliant collage that depicts enduring friendship, unconditional love, and spiritual fulfillment. I soar in an ocean with no water, ignited by an internal fire that is pure love. Immersed in this burning sea of Truth, I heed the inner voice that beckons me to boldly explore the universal path that the artist spoke of at our first encounter 13 years before.

Having seen a picture of Eckankar's leader that the artist carries with him, I ask him to tell me who this person

A New Path

is in his life. He describes his trust in this man whom he considers his best friend and confidant, explaining his connection to this ever-constant inner presence whose precious gift provides spiritual guidance.

Moved by the artist's poignant portrayal of his teacher, a powerful surge of energy wells up from within me. My heartbeat accelerates, my hands sweat and my body trembles. I must tell the artist the truth: his description of an "inner master" expresses my relationship with "the boy," a phenomenon that I've inwardly experienced for 22 years.

Inspired and determined to learn all that I can, I boldly decide to follow a new spiritual path. Now deceased, the founder of this worldwide organization has the same last name, Twitchell, as the family from whom we bought our summer home on the Cape, and the real estate agent who facilitated my discovery of the metal symbol with the letter "G" in the center.

* * *

While playing in a doubles match, a tennis friend invites my husband and me to a fortieth birthday party for her spouse. On a walk later that day I encounter our neighbor from the Boston suburbs who owns a beach house in the village. At the gas station on the corner of Main Street and School Street where I heard the second ethereal voice, I casually mention to her that we are invited to the upcoming celebration.

Visibly displeased, she grimaces and counters, "*You're* going to that party?"

A New Path

She then forbids me to become friends with a certain individual who will also attend this event and warns, "She's *my* friend and I don't want you to take her away from me."

Momentarily caught in an invisible torrent, my quivering body plummets into an ocean with no water. Submerged in the shadow of a memory from second grade, I see myself walking to school with several children from my neighborhood. Traipsing down the dirt road we pass the ball field behind my house, cross the busy main street and stop at the gas station to wait for the girl who lives in the adjacent house. When she comes outside, my next-door neighbor, a third-grader, leans into me and says, "I don't want you to talk to her. She's *my* friend, not yours."

* * *

In future years I notice other such unwarranted anxieties but I dismiss my apprehension. I choose to nurture a friendly rapport with this neighbor, even though she continues to place conditions on our ostensibly affable relationship. But one remark, a reference to her estranged friend, also my neighbor, haunts me: "I don't want her in our crowd. If you're my friend, you won't invite her to your Fourth of July party."

* * *

Twelve years after I place the metal symbol with the letter "G" in the center on a windowsill on our screened porch, my husband casually gives away the sign to the husband of the woman whose insecurity will eventually trigger the demise of our 21-year long association.

Characteristically unattached to material possessions, I am secretly distraught to see the metal symbol taken from its time-honored home on our screened porch. An incomprehensible force renders me helpless; I cannot move or speak. My heart pounds and my body trembles as this visceral response penetrates to the core of my being.

In this daunting moment, I am unaware of the obscured truth – my truth – locked away inside of me that so powerfully evokes my distress.

Come to Houston

Gillette Castle is a medieval-style attraction that overlooks the Connecticut River. The stage actor who originally portrayed Sherlock Holmes at the turn of the twentieth century designed this stone and wood residence with built-in furniture, hidden mirrors, secret passageways and intricately carved door latches that unlock like puzzles.

In high school, on a self-guided tour of this castle with my grandparents and my future husband, I ascend the open stairway that leads to the second floor. Just before I reach the landing I feel lightheaded and dizzy. As I pause to regain my equilibrium, I inwardly see a luminous vision of a small, sparsely furnished bedroom. Mystified, I stroll down the hallway and enter a room, a physical manifestation of the picture that had just flashed in my imagination.

* * *

At the end of the first summer in our beach house on the Cape, my family and I return to our home in the Boston suburbs. While I settle my children into a new school year I remain preoccupied with the stirring pronouncement, *Your patience is rewarded.*

I steal quiet moments to practice the spiritual exercises that the artist introduced me to at our first encounter 13 years ago. As I experiment with variations of this daily ritual, an avenue to accessing the space that opens when I close my eyes, I center on the inner whirring and garner messages from beyond.

In contemplation I wonder, *Is all of this real?*

A man's gentle voice responds, *Yes, as real as anything can be.*

I ask silently, *What more can I do to serve?*

The voice replies, *Love him.*

I inwardly expound, *I understand about the form but there's more…*

The voice interrupts my explication and interjects, *It's okay. He loves you, too. Come to Houston.*

I rouse from this transcendent bliss with a sense of urgency, an essential need to expel the gestating expansion that inhabits me. Shaken, I stumble to my desk and grope for a pen. I attempt to express this delicate conception, an ethereal aspect of my self, but I lack a vocabulary to cohesively explain this elusive phenomenon, inaudible to human ears and invisible to human eyes.

I compose an essay that seeks to give voice to the ineffable. As I write, a continual question irks me: *If not "the boy," then whose voice spoke to me?*

Dismissing this point, I return to my established patterns and preconceived notions. I elaborate upon the artist's capacity for inner knowing and his potential to be an influential spiritual leader in this lifetime. I then slide this confidential communiqué underneath the contents of my dresser drawer and crawl back into bed.

Three nights later I dream that I am alone in a hotel room in Houston. Communing with "the boy" in my inner sanctuary, I succumb to the blazing fire of desire that epitomizes my love of God. Here I inwardly entreat, *Marry me – the way you know how – right here, right now.*

In this mystical vision, a fervent petition for divine unity, the echo of my own voice resounds, *It's right. I know it is.*

My physical body convulses as I awaken from this dream and attempt to reorient my senses. I rise out of bed, slip into old clothes and lace up my running shoes. Spellbound, I jog on meandering roads that loop back to my home, anticipating the light of dawn.

By mid-morning I feel compelled to mail the illustrative letter that I concealed in my dresser drawer three days before. Home from the post office, I collapse on the couch in the upstairs den. In stillness my attention rests upon my intimate conversation with the artist on our drive from Provincetown to Boston the previous month. I relive the moment of implicit trust when I informed him that his description of the "inner master" expresses my relationship with "the boy."

This memory plunges me into the past where I re-enter a scene from my childhood. As my father lay unconscious on the living room couch in the big house above the family store, I know that I am called to be the helper. When the doctor arrives I walk out the back door, wander into the garden, and make a bargain. I offer my life so that my father could live. In this reenactment I hear my child voice pray, *What more can I do to serve?*

Come to Houston

Hours later, emerging from this distant memory, my mind floods with a barrage of truth-seeking queries: *Who am I? Why do I hear voices inside of me? Am I a messenger? Am I here to inform the artist of his spiritual significance?*

I pry myself off the couch and attempt to stand, but I faint and slump to the floor. I come to when I hear my children open the mud hall door, walk up the stairs, and rummage for snacks in the kitchen.

* * *

The next morning I conclude that I must challenge my fate. I summon the resolve to roll out of bed, get dressed, and trudge outdoors. I prod my body onward and transition into a faltering jog, resigned that the terms of my childhood bargain remain in effect, and certain that I can never turn back.

On the following day I have plans with my husband and children to attend a matinee performance of "Cats" at the Schubert Theater, but overburdened, I tell them that I cannot participate in this family excursion.

As I lay motionless on my bed, an electric shock spurts through my body. I don't understand why, but I intuitively know that I must rebuff my despair and accompany my family on this outing to Boston.

After the play, while my husband and children dine, I rest my forehead on the table. I look down and notice that my arms dangle just above my feet. I cannot yet fathom why I was compelled to exert such monumental effort to join in this outing. My family is worried about me, but I don't have the words to explain why I am in this weakened state.

On our way back to the parking garage the elevator unexpectedly stops between floors. Containing my own claustrophobia, I reassure my frightened daughter that we have plenty of air to breathe and that someone will soon come to help us get unstuck. As I comfort my oldest child I simultaneously hear the inner message, *Today the elevator, tomorrow the snake.*

The next day, on a walk with my son to a neighbor's house, a black snake slithers from a pile of damp leaves and curls up on a sun-drenched rock.

Later in the afternoon, feeling weary and troubled, I hike into Rocky Woods, a 500-acre reservation near my home. Drawn to this sacred refuge where the artist and I once walked together, I perch on the scenic ledge that overlooks the Boston skyline. Here, One with nature, I pray.

Ravaged by years of harboring my guarded inner secret, having confided only in the artist, I long to be free of the escalating fear that my concealed interior life will be exposed. Estranged from the child who coexisted harmoniously in both worlds, I'm torn between my earthly commitments and my divine calling. Distanced from center I await my imminent death, a welcome passage that I believe will eradicate the torment of my conflicted existence.

The Painting

As inner peace and tranquility continue to elude me, I reverberate with a persistent echo of the mysterious voice that conveyed the ethereal invitation, *Come to Houston.*

On the phone with the artist a week later, we speak about the upcoming Eckankar seminar. Thirteen years since he first mentioned Eckankar, an individual path to God, I tell him that I will also be at this meeting.

He promises, "It will be an adventure."

* * *

In Houston on the eve of this three-day event, I call the artist and invite him to my hotel room. Committed to a life of service since childhood, I confide in him that when I mailed my letter to him, I believe I've met my ultimate task as helper in this life seeking to give voice to something ineffable that's come to me: his capacity for inner knowing and his potential to be an influential spiritual leader at this time.

I share my darkest desire: I want to die. I believe I've exhausted my usefulness in this world. I try to conceal my deeper truth: I can no longer endure the agony of my conflicted existence nor the torment of unrequited love.

Kindhearted, the artist suggests that my soul assignment likely encompasses far more than delivering a single message, perhaps to give testimony, to share my truth with others.

Just a girl from Thompsonville, I flinch at this notion. I tell myself that my truth is obscured, locked away in

The Painting

a chamber deep inside of me. I keep secrets even from myself. I'm neither worthy nor qualified to decipher the meaning of the mystical events that shape my life.

I acknowledge the sincerity of the artist's speculation, but deem myself unviable, powerless to embark upon the virtuous journey that he imagines.

As fear and self-doubt vie for my attention, I question my motive for attending this seminar at all, why I resolved to heed the inner directive, *Come to Houston.*

* * *

The next morning I swarm among thousands of participants at the Houston Convention Center. From an extensive list of activities and group discussions, I choose one particular topic that beckons me: *how to overcome the negativity that can pervade the mind.*

I linger outside the designated meeting room, feeling hesitant to cross the threshold. Without knowing why, I reverse direction and walk away from the entrance. Disoriented, I gaze into the amorphous crowd that approaches. A visceral urge to flee overcomes me but I can't move.

My eyes focus upon one individual, and the artist joins me. In this large-group discussion I learn about witnessing, self-examining, and neutralizing my negative thoughts.

When the session ends I stand near the artist in a wide, crowded corridor and intermittently join in conversations

The Painting

with his friends. I feel the embrace of unconditional love, acceptance and camaraderie within this conscious community.

As throngs of truth-seekers file by, a tall, distinguished older gentleman emerges from the crowd. Facing me, he peers into my eyes and humbly states that he knows me. When I respond that I don't recall meeting him, the stranger explains that he's seen me in his dreams.

Puzzled, I play down his comment and continue to wait for the artist. Moments later a woman I don't know, a soft-spoken brunette, approaches me and says that she's met me before. Like the man who has just spoken to me, she tells me that she sees me in her dreams. When a third person materializes from the group and reports this same occurrence, I secretly dissolve in a symphony of inner whirring that repeatedly intones, *Is all of this real?*

* * *

In the afternoon I venture into a small-group forum on living a life of soul. When the conversation turns to overcoming fears, I feel electrified. In the final segment of this discussion I muster the courage to speak up and share how I remained composed when stuck in an elevator one day and again the next when confronted with a snake on my path. But my impulse backfires. The facilitator interrupts me and announces that I've had my chance to speak. He then monopolizes the remaining time to deliver his prepared closing remarks.

The Painting

Mortified, I invisibly slip into the space that opens when I close my eyes. Here, in the safety of my inner sanctuary, I remember that the artist is the only one who understands me, the only person I can trust. I realize I must wait for inner guidance before I take my next step.

Overcome with fatigue, I return to my hotel room and fall into bed. In stillness, the inner whirring intensifies. I sink deeper into an ocean with no water and in this vast space peace and tranquility envelop and replenish me.

* * *

Rested, I rejoin the thousands of seekers at the Houston Convention Center for the evening session of the seminar. As I sit by myself at the back of the huge room, a friend of the artist rushes toward me. The exuberant woman grasps my arm, pulls me to my feet and exclaims, "I've been looking for you. Come with me. I saved a seat for you. This is your first seminar. You have to sit up front."

Before the program begins I sense the rising momentum of the group dynamic. Inspirational music augments the fervor as the anticipation builds. Well into the presentation, the keynote speaker appears on stage and the zeal of the audience erupts.

With his first uttered syllable the leader of Eckankar commands everyone's attention. Listening to the cadence of his gentle voice, I drift into the essence of my childhood, see the brilliant colors and geometric patterns of my first kaleidoscope and hear the reverberation of the helicopter

The Painting

that once landed in my backyard. The interior whirring revs to an invigorating frequency, an intoxicating vibration that both carries me far away and draws me in close.

Captivated, I identify a familiar chord in the amplified voice of the presenter on center stage. The distinctive tonal quality projects through the charged air, and I recognize the vocal pattern that instructed me to, "Come to Houston."

I feel further enlivened when the leader of Eckankar speaks about a woman afraid of snakes who confronted one in her yard. When he posits that when we ask for something, we usually get it right away – positive or negative – I ponder how this applies to me.

* * *

On the ride back to the hotel I sit next to the artist in the open-air bed of a pickup truck. Talking with his friends, I flow with the rhythm of his soothing words and inwardly resonate with the sound of his familiar voice. Attentive to the natural whirring and the burning desire that emanate from within me, I simultaneously feel connected and distant; comforted and tormented.

The sincerity of the artist's conversation among friends reminds me of my inner communication with "the boy" and evokes memories of our intimate exchanges about friendship, forgiveness, surrender and divine love. But, I'm reluctant to join in their conversation. I'm terrified that if I speak candidly, I may inadvertently expose my concealed interior life.

The Painting

Seeking refuge, I enter the infinite space that is my private sanctuary. In a world that is hidden from the outside but visible to me from the inside, I am cloaked in darkness and drenched in light. In the stillness of this curative realm I release harmful influences that may inhibit my potential. Empty, I explode into a sea of calm, disintegrate into wholeness, and fill with revitalizing energy.

This is my center, the far-away domain where I replenish my soul and rejuvenate my spirit. Here, in my deepest self, where only truth resides, I am complete, free to welcome death and to embrace life.

Traveling back to the hotel in the pick-up truck, I am fraught with unanswerable questions and ambivalent feelings. The profundity of this inward journey disturbs and intrigues me. To preserve my sanity I assume a persona, a genuine guise of affability that I customarily wear to mask my internal chaos and conceal my innermost truth, especially from myself.

Inhaling the night air, I silently pray for inner strength, asking for help to allay my greatest fear: my guarded inner secret will be revealed. I also ask for relief from the agony of unrequited love. I ask to remain open, calm, and centered for the duration of my earthly journey. *May I have the fortitude to comply with the terms of my childhood bargain*, I petition. *I am willing to give up my life in service for love.* I whisper aloud the cryptic message that comes as response: *I'm working on it.*

* * *

The Painting

At the hotel the artist invites me to join him and his friends at an informal gathering. We meet in a small room where an easel stands draped in a dark cloth, concealing a canvas underneath. He talks with his companions about the art of color-seeing and the process of creating light, announcing to the group that he will now present a special gift to a friend.

When he removes the fabric covering and unveils his work, I am shocked. The roar of inner whirring consumes me. I lower my trembling body onto the edge of the bed for support. Sheathed in my persona, I disengage from my surroundings and dissolve into my self.

The resplendent painting, radiant with the light of inner knowing, echoes my inner visions. The artist's composition contains all of the elements that I see in my imagination: the boy, the fence, the pasture, the horse, the rays of sunlight, the semblance of an inner guide, but it's the energy that emanates from the painting that overwhelms me. The artist's creation, a physical manifestation of my innermost reality, captures the essence of my guarded inner secret.

At first, I feel exposed and violated, stripped of my voice and my free will. I invisibly drown in a flood of repressed emotion and unleashed fear, slipping further into my external persona.

My spirit soars as I merge with the inner whirring and the sparkling lights of my childhood kaleidoscope. I feel the presence of "the boy" with whom I've shared my secreted existence. Gazing through a lens of unconditional love,

The Painting

I view the painting as testament to the pure and innocent connection that the artist and I embody, an unbreakable bond of freedom that eternally unites us as One.

I realize that only *I* am aware of the obscured meaning of the painting and its profound impact upon me. Only *I* know that when the artist unveiled the painting, he revealed my guarded inner secret. Only *I* understand that the painting's special gift, remarkable because the painting was not intended for me, has allowed me to confront my greatest fear and face my true self. I return to my hotel room, pick up a pen, and write in my personal journal…

* * *

When I complete this entry that I address to the artist but write for myself, I hide my private journal for safekeeping and crawl into bed. Throughout the night my awakened body palpitates in a conscious state of alertness and receptivity. The amplified interior whirring fixes my attention while the luminosity of inner knowing infiltrates my being. At daybreak I call the artist and ask him to come to my hotel room to talk with me about an important spiritual matter that is of value to both of us.

Inwardly guided, I explain to him the underlying significance of the painting that he presented to his friend the evening before. I describe my psychological response, the sense of exposure I felt, when I saw his unveiled painting. I express my appreciation for this artistic rendering, which, for me, serves to authenticate our deep connection, substantiate

The Painting

our interior communication, and validate my interior existence.

I share how tenaciously I've guarded my inner secret and clung to my greatest fear. Able to confide only in him, I confess that I would rather die than expose my concealed truth. But his painting allowed me to survive the unthinkable, the unveiling of my interior existence.

Alone, forced to confront the fear of facing my true self, I am transformed. I realize that what I perceived as my imminent death is not a literal departure from the physical world but an internal transition, a radical yet imperceptible change in perspective that will eventually allow me to trust my inner knowing and prepare me to meet my destiny.

I recognize that my awakened consciousness is both an ending and a beginning.

I learn that beliefs proliferated from the outside are distinct from and less trustworthy than truths that germinate from center. On this circuitous journey to and from center I reverberate with the reminder that when we ask for something, we usually get it right away.

* * *

Trust in God and no one else.
Your patience is rewarded.

* * *

Home from the Seminar

Home in the Boston suburbs after the worldwide seminar in Houston, I appear to be the same, but I am forever changed. I know I can never turn back. As I return to the demands of daily life and family responsibilities, I am sleep-deprived but feel wired and wide awake. A well deep inside of me recharges my body and stimulates my inner awareness.

Musing, I review the life-altering events that have occurred in the preceding three days. I envision the painting that the artist unveiled among friends only 48 hours before. I marvel that this gift, an unintentional representation of my guarded inner secret, allowed me to confront my ultimate fear and face my true self. I inwardly replay tapes of inspiring conversations at the seminar about creativity, forgiveness, healing, love and the desire to serve. I hear the resounding symphony of bells, trumpets and violins that emerged from within as I participated in a culminating activity, an all-consuming vocal chant.

But now that I'm home, distanced from the charged atmosphere of the seminar, fear and self-doubt undermine my elation. As I lay awake throughout the night, an onslaught of discombobulated words and scrambled messages bombard my senses and assail my mind. Inundated with rapid-fire pulsations, I try to slow down the input, but I cannot decode the transmissions that race through my body.

Home from the Seminar

Believing that this flow of information will one day serve a purpose, I know intuitively that I must harness the information that speeds through me and just as quickly disintegrates into oblivion. Inwardly directed, I rise out of bed, pick up a pen and write, *Please help me to put these words down on paper.*

An inexplicable force guides my hand as I write, *Be persistent and obey. Write what you hear coming through your body. Trust completely in God.*

* * *

Four days after the seminar ends I remain in a state of high receptivity. I record messages in my journal that come through my senses and details from my dreams. Oblivious to my physical exhaustion, I dissolve into the climactic energy until it cracks open a foggy window and gives me a glimpse into my inner world.

I probe deeper, asking a familiar question, *Is all of this real?*

And receive the same answer, *Yes, as real as anything can be.*

Uncertain, I press on, *What more can I do to serve?*

Love him.

But now, emerging from the shadow of this pregnant response, I hear an addendum…

We have arrived at the heart of the matter, the highest expression of love in appreciation of God.

Hearing this I pick up a pen and address a journal entry to Chuck…

Home from the Seminar

...It's unlikely that two lives will ever again come together in exactly the same way that our lives are together. Our relationship is very special and unique, and can never be duplicated.

Finally able to sleep, I have a vivid dream. I walk out of an empty room and enter into an expansive corridor. In slow motion I turn to watch the artist exit the same room. With tears streaming down his face, he approaches me and gazes into my eyes. I hold him close.

When I awaken I realize that the inner conflict in this dream is a reflection of my own internal strife, my struggle to reconcile my spiritual path with the demands of my everyday existence. As the pressure builds I turn to writing to help release my mounting tension, but this alone cannot balance the overload of energy. Asking again for help, I listen to the inner voice.

Use this energy to open the way for anyone you can reach. Making a commitment to God is not enough. Understanding how you are meant to serve and knowing the direction to take is the solidification, the confirmation of this commitment. One day, when you are ready, these writings will serve a purpose. But, more importantly, these words are intended to assist in touching the lives of souls through the power of the Holy Spirit.

* * *

One month after the seminar in Houston, my life may appear perfectly ordered, but to spiritually progress I must pay close attention to the emerging patterns on this circuitous journey. I reaffirm my commitment to unlock any truth that I conceal from myself.

Home from the Seminar

As I write in my journal I am oblivious to the sound coming from the television in the family room. Then, as if an invisible hand suddenly turns up the volume, I distinctly hear the actor, John Ritter, share a piece of advice that he received from his parents: "Do something with your life that is bigger than yourself."

This statement triggers a brilliant flash within me where I see a wide perspective of life, a vantage point radiates Time's continuum from inception throughout all eternity – all in a single moment. Rapt in this light of inner knowing, I recollect the words that the gardener in Ogunquit spoke to me 16 years before when I was a newlywed: *God will always be with you.*

* * *

In stillness, just before I fall asleep that evening, I hear the gentle message: *Listen with your heart.* Then, in a dream, a woman that I don't know tells me I must think more deeply in order to help those in need. As she softly rests her index finger upon the center of her forehead, she whispers to me: *It comes from here first.*

In the dream I see myself on an indoor tennis court about to begin a new game. Before I serve the ball I notice that a fence stands on my side of the court and blocks my vision, but I serve the ball anyway. After I twice fail to clear the fence, I walk onto the court and move the fence out of the way. When I serve the tennis ball this time, it lands in the service box.

* * *

Home from the Seminar

On the eighth of December, the day that the Catholic Church observes the Feast of the Immaculate Conception, I dream that my body soars above the treetops, marveling at the aerial view of Big Sur, California. I land on the ground, get into a car, and drive to a town where a street vendor sells shoes. I walk through a doorway and enter a white room where rows of brown church pews face one another. Dozens of children sit on the wooden benches and cry because they can't find their shoes, while other children frantically sort through mountains of mismatched footwear.

When I awaken I record the dream in my journal. As I write, I recognize an urgent need to express all that resides within me. I address extensive entries to Chuck, but I do not yet share my private commentaries with him. Journaling is a life-saving practice for me, where I can safely express myself and explore my spiritual growth. As I learn to accept the inner knowing that springs from the divine, my writing teaches me to trust myself.

* * *

Trust in God and no one else.

* * *

During the night a mighty wave of prolific energy swells inside of me. Gripped in this upsurge, my heart pounds in my chest as I grasp a pen, steady my hand and release the explosion of words that emerges through intuitive dictation.

Home from the Seminar

The only way to heal oneself is to confront the issue...let go of the emotions of the past...look inwardly for the solutions to all dilemmas....

For weeks I document the transmissions that come through my body. I feel energized as I transcribe the plethora of material that flows onto the written page. Although I can't explain what generates these productive episodes, I remind myself that I requested help to *put these words down on paper.*

When this period of high receptivity ebbs, I study the spontaneous writings that I have been given. The collection of didactic information reads like a map, a lifelong course of action for me to follow. The lessons spiral through topics such as letting go of the past, divine imagination, self-motivation, spiritual missions, accepting the challenge, relinquishing control, divine love, the nature of God, formlessness, paradox, the art of communication and creativity.

* * *

We have arrived at the heart of the matter, the highest expression of love in appreciation of God.

* * *

Opening to the Mystery, I trust that one day I will emerge from the darkness of my metaphoric womb, awaken to my fertility and give birth to my true Self.

The Key

In a recurring dream I stroll in darkness along the ocean's edge, illumined by the reflected light of the evening moon. A man clad in a long, hooded robe stands on the gradient slope of the sandy beach. From a distance, he gazes upon me with knowing eyes. As gentle waves roll onto the shore beneath my feet, I feel that he has come to protect me.

Weeks later, in a packet of information I receive from Eckankar, I see the sketch of an alleged spiritual teacher, a man who appears to be the figure that comes in my dreams.

* * *

Four months since the seminar in Houston, I lay awake and replay the mysterious events that have shaped my life. Searching, I wonder if my unique experiences may guide me toward my destiny. Yet overwhelmed by the challenge of reconciling my earthly commitments and my divine calling, I subliminally wish that I had died under the rolling wheels of the tractor-trailer truck when I was a child.

Without warning, a bolt of electrifying energy rockets my body out of this haze. Fueled by a pregnant impulse, I spring out of bed, grab a pen from my desk and write, *When have I paid enough? How much pain is too much? When does the suffering stop?*

And the immediate reply, *To ask the question is to know the answer.*

* * *

The Key

For days I fixate upon this cryptic response but I'm not yet able to decipher its meaning. Drained, I curl up on the couch in the upstairs den to watch a movie.

When the video recording of *Splash* begins I identify with the characters, a boy and a girl, who swim together in an underwater world. Reminiscent of floating with "the boy" in an ocean with no water, this opening scene captures my attention and pierces my heart.

Again confronted with a visual representation of my innermost reality, I relive the moment when the artist unveiled the painting that exposed my guarded inner secret. As I focus on the mesmerizing inner dance, the movement of geometric shapes and brilliant colors in my first kaleidoscope, a crescendo of interior whirring reminds me that to spiritually mature, I must study the recurring steps, the repetitive patterns that have emerged on my life's circuitous journey.

* * *

Over the weekend I attend a conference in Boston. In a workshop about dreams, the facilitator instructs the participants to close their eyes and visualize a horse. My imagination takes me to a grassy meadow with a palomino tacked in a Western saddle and bridle. In the background, gold stars illumine an image of Eckankar's spiritual leader. In concert with this image, I hear a distinct voice declare, *The key is love.*

The Key

Though immersed in this spontaneous revelation I remain aware of the facilitator's rambling drone pronouncing each subsequent instruction: visualize accessories on the horse....place yourself in the picture....envision the inner master surrounded by a golden light....ask him for *the key*....

* * *

During a break in the program I approach a fellow attendee and say, "Hi, Alan. Remember me? I'm Paula. We met in Houston."

The young man acknowledges my greeting but tells me that he wasn't in Houston last fall. He was in Mexico. He then adds that though he couldn't directly attend the worldwide seminar, he entered into contemplation and visualized being there.

Speechless, I recall the mystifying phenomenon that occurred in Houston after I attended my first session, a discussion about the negativity that can pervade the mind. As I relive the moment when fellow truth-seekers tell me they've seen me in their dreams, I dissolve in the swirling shadow of a recurrent question: *Is all of this real?*

* * *

At home in the Boston suburbs, I open the mail and read detailed information about a seminar that will take place in Anaheim, California, in the spring. I long to attend this event but I'm torn. On the same weekend my family will celebrate Easter and my grandmother's eighty-fifth birthday.

The Key

Resigned to accept my fate, I deal with this scheduling conflict by rationalizing that a cross-country trip to California would be prohibitively expensive.

In a phone conversation the following day, my mother outlines the plans for our family party. As I listen, a swift current of entangled verbiage sweeps me into the beyond. Here I unite with a pulsating energy that rises from the depths of my being. At the pinnacle of this liberating wave, I give voice to the fire that burns in my heart.

Unscripted, I express my interpretation of this compelling interior decree: "I will not be at the family celebration on Easter Sunday because I'm going to an Eckankar seminar in California."

After this spontaneous declaration I backpedal to answer the barrage of questions that follows. Dutiful, I explain to my mother that I'm exploring a new spiritual path that doesn't follow a traditional religious calendar. I tell her that I relate to others on this path and resonate with the content of related books that I read. I add that I sometimes encounter specific passages that describe my own personal life experiences.

My mother is stunned but restrained.

As I hang up the phone my heart pounds and my body trembles. Transformed, I am mindful of my call to courage, to expand beyond the rules, beyond fear and self-doubt, to unlock my truth and experience the fullness of life.

The Key

But as the energy settles I think about the family gathering that I will miss and the disappointment that my absence will inflict upon those I love. Sorting through my compunction, I grieve over the loss of the life that I've known. As I enter a new portal, I am aware that I may never turn back.

Stymied in the fray between my earthly bonds and my divine calling, I pray: *What's the next step?*

And out of stillness I hear: *The way is not always easy, but it's the only way. Fear not. Only love. You will be okay. Love is the only way to the Supreme Being. Love is always with you. Love is waiting for you.*

* * *

I dream that I give up all that I have: my life, my home, my husband, my children – all for the love of God. Alone, I'm overcome with feelings of abandonment and dread. Here, in darkness and gloom, I cast a life sentence upon myself: to forever dwell in this eternal wasteland.

In the shadow of timeless despair, I wait. Imprisoned in this barren realm I imagine that an ethereal breeze whispers to me: *love will sustain you….love is the answer….let go of everything else….let go of it all….*

But in this dream, the dreamer clings to the certainty that this glimmer of hope is only an illusion.

* * *

When I awaken I feel disoriented, inept, and plagued with uncertainty. Determined to rebound, I force myself out of bed, dress in running clothes and trudge outdoors. Pressing forward I break into a slow jog, but each step is a grueling effort.

The Key

On a familiar street a mile from home a faint gurgling sound beckons me. Curious, I trace this audible lifeline to its source, a natural spring in a nearby yard. Suspended in time, I unite with the clarity and potency of the healing flow that bubbles from the earth. One with this life-affirming force, I intuitively know that this auspicious sign calls me to my destiny.

At home with my husband I share my fervent desire to attend the upcoming spring seminar in Anaheim, even though the trip will be costly. In response to my dilemma, my husband opens his attaché case and hands me two reward certificates, one for round trip airfare and the other for a three-night stay at any Marriott Hotel.

* * *

Grateful, I contemplate the timeless observation that when we ask for something, it usually comes right away. In stillness, I realize that to *ask* is to raise awareness, to be conscious of the need to nurture and protect the seed of inner knowing yet to germinate and grow to fruition. *To be receptive is to be patient and open, to hear the call to love and honor the willingness to serve.*

And to *know* is not a function of the mind, but a fullness of the heart.

* * *

To ask the question is to know the answer.

* * *

Familiar Passages

On a winter day in 1988, I curl up with a book written by the spiritual leader of Eckankar. I'm learning that this spiritual path is intended to increase one's awareness of self and of the divine through everyday experiences. I read about a man who in his youth was chased by rabbit-like animals with red eyes. I picture the white creatures that snapped at my heels when I was a child and remember running down the hill behind my house so fast that my feet would barely touch the ground.

The man whose experience reminds me of mine is the founder of Eckankar, now deceased. He has the same last name, Twitchell, as the real estate agent who facilitated the purchase of our summer home on the Cape, which led to the discovery of the metal symbol with the letter "G" in its center that my children playfully imagined stood for our last name, Gowdy. I later discover that it is a unique symbol of the Freemasons.

When I arrive at an eerily familiar passage that echoes very similar pivotal events in my own life, I plunge into the past. I relive the moment when my mother vowed to never forgive me if I ever told my father the truth about my sister's baby. I also remember how my uncle wrongly blamed me for my mother's unhappiness and recall, too, the betrayal of a supposed friend who accused me of lying when I was telling the truth.

Familiar Passages

As my heart races and my body trembles, I return to the book that speaks to spiritual mastership and reread the passage that describes a woman who, as a child, was caught between her mother and her father and blamed for things that she did not do.

Opening to the mystery of this synchronicity, I resonate with the essential spirit of this enigma. Enlivened, I embody the words that my grandmother shared with me when I was a teenager: "Nothing new ever happens in this world. People have the same experiences over and over again."

* * *

On family vacation with my husband and children, I dash through the Magic Kingdom at Disney World, eager to climb aboard the Big Thunder Mountain Railroad. As I wind my way to this rollicking roller coaster, I notice the name, Chuck, plastered in various sites in the amusement park. I see the name on a menu board, on a tee shirt, on a brown wooden barrel, on a colorful banner, and on the back of a raft that floats in the water. Each time I encounter this name I pause in wonderment.

Waiting in line for the roller coaster, I inch forward on an elevated platform and weave through a grid of successive turns. As I consider the recurrent sightings of this evocative name, I reach a wide opening where I stop to gaze upon the scene below. Energized by the multitude that swarms in the park, I fill with an overwhelming desire to focus on every face in the crowd, to recognize each individual as a unique being, a valued soul.

That afternoon, on my way to the dizzying Mad Tea Party, I stop to browse in one of the many Disney gift shops. Empty-handed, I exit the store and merge into a stream of park visitors. Dazzled in the brilliant sunlight, I hear an inquiring voice call my name.

Reunited with a high school friend who now lives in Florida, I take a moment to catch my breath and reorient my senses. Seated on a curved wall that surrounds a vibrant flower garden, I recollect the day that I last saw this classmate. Fourteen years ago she came to an intimate gathering at my home after we attended the funeral of a dear friend, a young woman who was abducted during a bank robbery and murdered.

When I return from Florida I call my girlfriend, the person who introduced me to my husband in high school, to tell her about my surprising encounter with our mutual friend. The moment I mention her name she gasps and asks eagerly, "What day did you see her?"

Shopping at a store in our hometown on that same Saturday, my girlfriend had turned the corner of an aisle and come upon the parents of our deceased classmate. Unable to face them, she had panicked and fled.

That night I lay awake in animated stillness. As a gestating energy erupts from the pregnant calm I acknowledge again the enduring truth that we are all One.

Familiar Passages

* * *

I continue to contemplate the passages in the Eckankar book that seize my attention. I think to myself: *Does the author realize that he's woven into his story a set of circumstances that has been lived by another?*

Reaching for my pen, I compose a letter in which I ask the spiritual leader of Eckankar to explain why the experiences he recounts are so similar to mine. Instead of mailing this inquiry, I tuck it into the pages of a spiral notebook, the private journal where I record my innermost secrets.

Focused on my life-affirming writing practice that allows me to explore my truth, the intuitive knowing that I believe springs from the divine, I notice an incongruity. Trusting my higher Self, I address extensive journal entries to Chuck, but yielding to my fear and self-doubt, I conceal these writings from him.

As I examine this contradiction in my patterned behavior, I acknowledge that writing is an essential outlet that helps to relieve my internal pressure, but I'm not yet able to integrate the dynamic voice that speaks directly to me. By channeling these writings to Chuck, I subconsciously cushion the impact of facing the unknown, to protect myself from the secrets that are locked inside of me. Still convinced of his potential to become an influential spiritual leader in this lifetime, I'm unable to see that my writings project my visions onto Chuck, because I'm not yet ready to accept them as my own.

Delving deeper, I realize that it's time for me to take an active step to further my own spiritual development. To facilitate my own growth, I must free myself and move toward harmonizing my inner and outer worlds. Aware that my choices in life are catalysts for change, I now understand that I must summon the courage to heed my natural instinct and share with Chuck the detailed writings that I both address to and conceal from him.

But, where past and present meet in the here and now, I struggle with my essential complex issue: facing my true self. I again contemplate the questions that surfaced three years ago when the powerful interior directive, *Trust in God and no one else*, compelled me to unearth my guarded inner secret: *Do I have the right to impose upon him? Is revealing my truth in his best interest? Will he think I'm crazy?*

* * *

At the end of March 1988, I arrive in Anaheim, California, to attend the spring Eckankar seminar. I meet several individuals with whom I experience instantaneous connections.

As I browse through music selections in the book room, a woman holds up a cassette tape and comments, "This is beautiful. You should listen to it sometime." She then introduces herself and adds, "I was drawn to you. I just had to talk to you." I quickly discover that we both chose the same three workshops to attend from a lengthy list of offerings. I also learn that she plans to move thousands of miles from home to relocate in Massachusetts. A few weeks later my new acquaintance is an overnight guest at our house in the Boston suburbs.

When I walk into a spacious meeting room I notice a woman sitting alone at a table. I intuitively ask if I may join her. As we talk, she confides that she is skeptical about Eckankar and that she doubts the reality of the inner experiences that people describe. Empathetic with her concerns, I tell her about the voice that beckoned me to *come to Houston* last fall. Like two old friends, we sit together that night at the evening session of the seminar.

The following morning, standing alone in the crowded hotel lobby, I feel a wave of pure energy wash over me as a woman passes by. When I spontaneously reach for her hand, she embraces me. Engaged in a four-hour conversation that night, I describe the events in my life that led me to Eckankar, and she tells me about the inner workings of the organization. As we talk, she asks why I reached out to her in the hotel lobby. She then explains that while waiting outside, she heard a voice call for her to come inside. When she did, guidance led her to me.

* * *

The key is love.

* * *

One night I lie in bed and contemplate the question I raised in the letter I addressed to the spiritual leader of Eckankar before tucking it into the pages of a spiral notebook. *Why are the experiences he recounts in his book so similar to mine?*

Resounding with a crescendo of inner whirring that awakens my body, I explode with an intoxicating aliveness. As I attempt to reconcile my resonance with Eckankar's leader's experience, a direct response to my inquiry erupts from deep within.

So you will accept it. You know what is real but you still question. You still doubt. Accept it completely and live it every moment of your life.

As I hear myself counter, *But...*

An emphatic voice interrupts, *Accept it. Stop resisting. You know it's all true. You know it's real. Enjoy it.*

Opening to the vibrations that pulse from center, I view this enigmatic exchange as I would a painting or a poem. I delve into its composition and align with the rhythm of the creative process that revitalizes my body and adds meaning to my existence. Woven into the fabric of this mystery I recognize a pattern: every answer is a new beginning, an opening into a new question.

My thoughts return to the unnamed woman in the book about spiritual mastery. *Who is this woman whose life shines a light upon mine?*

Grateful for the Love

Sitting at my desk in homeroom, I look up at the clock and realize that I'm late for a meeting. A senior in high school, I'm on a committee to help organize a town-wide fundraiser for a scholarship foundation. I approach the teacher and ask for permission to report to the office, but he ignores me. I watch him shuffle piles of papers on his desk.

While I wait for a response, the intercom buzzes. I recognize the school secretary's voice as she asks the educator to send me to the office.

In slow motion the teacher turns his head toward me and glares. In a burst of anger he unleashes a stream of cutting remarks. He professes that I think I'm so important that this school can't exist without me. With contempt he roars, "Just who do you think you are?"

I feel my throat burn as I fight to restrain the tears. An eternity passes before the teacher dismisses me with a wave of his hand and growls, "Go. I don't care what you do."

Humiliated, I travel an endless distance to navigate my way out of the classroom. I tell myself that I must be strong, that I must counter this insult and work to accomplish the worthwhile task that's been assigned to me.

* * *

In March 1988, before I leave for the spring Eckankar seminar in Anaheim, California, my husband reads the

Grateful for the Love

journal entries in the spiral notebooks that I have secured with tape and hidden in my bureau drawer. Empathetic with his confusion and pain, I desperately want him to know the real me, to accept me as I am. But when I try to explain my account of a spiritual marriage, a mystical experience that can bring wholeness and divine unity, I cannot find the words to convey the sanctity of this interior phenomenon.

Two days later my husband suffers a severe migraine headache. Personally familiar with this debilitating disorder, I silently pray for his symptoms to subside. When I hear him call my name, I perch on the edge of the bed and ask him what he needs. He utters a few words, but abruptly stops before he completes a sentence.

Moments later he tells me that when I sat down next to him the pain and nausea disappeared, and now he feels fine, as if the episode had never occurred.

* * *

That week my mother arrives at our home in the Boston suburbs for a three-day visit. During a lengthy conversation she tells me that she agrees with everything that she's read in the Eckankar books that I had given to her. After I answer her questions about my decision to follow this new path, she admits that even though she's intrigued, she could never separate from her Catholicism, her religion since birth.

Grateful for the Love

Understanding the constraints that attachment and fear perpetuate, I reflect upon my gradual yet heart-wrenching departure from the Church, the religious tradition that shaped my childhood identity and kindled my faith.

As we talk my mother comments that she notices something different about me. Now 20 years since she threatened to never forgive me if I ever told my father the truth about the baby that my sister abandoned, she remarks, "You're very happy, aren't you? Happier than you've been in a long time."

Smiling, I nod in agreement.

Then she continues, "You're a good person. You've always been a good person, but you were hurt. You must have been hurt and angry for a long time. And now, as you put it, you've let it go."

Four years later my mother once again obliquely refers to our family fracture. Propped up on a hospital bed, dying of pancreatic cancer, she whispers to my sister and me, "All is forgiven."

Although my mother had never been able to tell me that she was sorry, I had forgiven her years before, aware that she felt justified in her actions against me. But, as life drains from her body, my heart aches as I wonder if she has ever forgiven herself for her transgressions.

* * *

In a dream I stand in the living room of the four-room ranch house where I lived as a child. My body occupies the same space where, when as a teenager, I witnessed my family's supreme evasion of truth when the stranger who came to our door announced that my sister had a baby.

Face to face with Chuck in the dream, I notice that the spiritual leader of Eckankar stands motionless beside him.

With outstretched arms I hold a long letter in front of me that I have composed. Reading aloud from this document, I inform Chuck that I cannot refer to this man as a living master. I listen to my own voice as I explain that an inner master is a presence that resides within, an accompanying state of being and an aspect of myself, an alter ego, the essence of my authentic Self.

Emerging from this dream I wonder if I had been awake or asleep when I envisioned this scene. Aware that I have doubts about my affiliation with Eckankar, I acknowledge to myself that I primarily joined Eckankar to ensure access to Chuck, my only support.

As I ponder my allusion to a living master, I revisit my concerns. I'm skeptical of a hierarchal system that elevates the status of its leader and encourages reliance upon an individual to access the depths of the interior self, the space that opens when I close my eyes. I'm also leery of a methodology that assigns a numerical ranking to the spiritual progress of participants in its organization.

Despite my reservations, I'm grateful for the unconditional love, acceptance and camaraderie exuded from the heart of this community. Certain that I will one day meet my destiny regardless of the path I follow, I regard my membership in this group as a stepping-stone, a springboard, for accelerating my ongoing process of self-discovery, my unrelenting quest for truth and meaning.

* * *

Mindful of my intention to free myself to move forward and bolster my own spiritual development, at the spring Eckankar seminar in Anaheim, California, I give Chuck the spiral notebooks in which I've recorded my private journal entries. Certain that I must follow my intuitive guidance and share these secreted writings, I entrust him with the details of my innermost existence, hopeful that this radical step will harmonize the outer with the inner and allow me to progress on my spiritual path. This extreme action symbolizes my unconditional love and implicit trust in him, while also acknowledging the trust that I must have in my Self. (For the next four years I continue to record my innermost truth in spiral notebooks that I secure in brown paper and mail to Chuck, my lifeline, my sole confidant.) Although relieved of the burden of keeping these writings to myself, I know that I'm not yet ready to share my innermost secrets with anyone else.

* * *

Home from the seminar, I return to my family and the demands of everyday life, but I feel inwardly disconcerted. Bombarded with unsettling dreams, I fret over my decision to risk my vulnerability and bare my truth. Sleep-deprived,

Grateful for the Love

I wage an interior battle to fend off the negative influences that undermine my confidence. Exhausted from weeks of inner turmoil, I stop writing in my journal, a practice that has consumed several hours of each day.

The following month, determined to overcome my limitations and align with my true self, I regain the energy to pick up my pen and resume journaling. As I re-establish this life-affirming routine I feel a shift in my perspective. Free of constraints, I imagine that my love and trust in Chuck reflect the same qualities that exist within all beings, including myself.

Awakened to a memory from my childhood, I visualize the little red berry that my father planted in earth and nurtured into a sturdy bush. I feel my father's love, the active ingredient that allowed this whisper of life to grow from a seed to its full potential. Love is the essential catalyst that fuels transformation and promotes the evolution of our universe.

* * *

The key is love.

* * *

Riding upon a wave of change, I open to the palpable vibrations that electrify my body and translate the rapid-fire pulsations into words on the written page. I contemplate the dynamic transmissions that came to me in August 1987 through divine guidance, the voice of my true Self:

Grateful for the Love

The day will come when the words you write will serve a purpose. The stories you tell will convey a message. This writing is not only for you; it's for everyone on the path. Cultivate this gift for the benefit of mankind to help others come to know the love that abounds.

Recognize the constant love and protection that is present. You must work hard to earn this state of awareness each day. Don't let up, not even for a moment. Love more deeply and surrender more fully. It is a matter of degree: the greater the love, the deeper the inner connection, the closer to center, the clearer you may hear the voice of guidance.

Your point of view and your range of abilities are widening every moment. Open yourself up to them. Let every vibration conceivable enter you, and then give it all back to the world. You have to keep that exchange open on a magnitude that far exceeds your personal life.

You will continue on this journey as far as it will take you, but never take it for granted. Never delude yourself into believing that you will reach your goal no matter what. You have to earn it. Do not get too comfortable. Work relentlessly. You may falter at times but you will not fail. Never settle for less than what you are chosen to be. But there is always a price to pay. Be prepared to give up whatever you must in order to have it all.

Bumps in the Road

In 1988, after sharing my private journals with the artist at the Eckankar seminar in Anaheim, California, I'm caught in crossfire. A 37-year-old mother of three, I battle to survive the volatile convergence of my everyday life and my secreted inner calling.

In a dream I fight my way through a violent windstorm. Alone, I seek shelter inside an old white house planted in the middle of a withered hayfield. This house is furnished but uninhabited.

Beyond the roar of swooping air and the menacing groan of the wooden structure, I hear someone call my name. I race across the living room and fling open the front door. I brace myself on the threshold and then step outside.

Exposed to the harsh elements I plod across the yard, a windblown wasteland. Walking on the crunchy hay I feel the dry earth beneath me and realize I'm barefoot. I turn around deliberately and trudge back to the house to put on my shoes.

Better equipped, I again venture outdoors but the raging wind pummels my body. I return to the house a second time to get a winter coat.

Now ready to face the storm, I trek outside for the third time. Determined to withstand the powerful gale, I inch forward, step by step, toward the voice that beckons me.

Bumps in the Road

* * *

That summer I participate in a culminating activity at Kings Grant, our local tennis club on the Cape. For me, playing in this tournament is more than a game – it's an opportunity to prove to myself that I'm ready to move on to the next level. Aware of the harmony that exists between my inner and outer worlds, I envision this challenge as a defining moment, not only an athletic accomplishment but also a symbol of my willingness to move forward with my spiritual development.

In the final round of the doubles competition my partner and I triumph in our division. But a few days before the next major event, the upcoming singles championship, I suffer a setback.

In my driveway I get out of the car, jump up onto the old fieldstone wall, a shortcut to my back steps, and lose my balance. Teetering, I try to regain my equilibrium but I can't stop the momentum of my body. Falling backward, I extend my left arm behind me, slam the car door on my hand, and break my little finger.

The day before the decisive match I tape the splinted finger to my ring finger and gear up for a short practice. Refusing medication, I rely upon the relaxation techniques learned for childbirth to distract my mind from the pain. On the court, in a state of wakeful meditation, I imagine that every ball connects with the strings of my racket, sails over the net and lands inbounds.

But with every movement, every stroke of the ball and ensuing vibration, the throbbing increases. To compensate I bend my left arm at the elbow and rest my swollen hand on my upper body. Right-handed, I return most balls with a forehand swing and, when necessary, I resort to using a one-handed backhand instead of switching to my customary two-handed grip.

In a final test of endurance I toss a ball high into the air and reach for it with my racket. As I execute this one practice serve, I reaffirm my intention for tomorrow's match, to make every shot count.

Early the next morning as I prepare for the seminal event, I feel my body open to a guiding presence. On the tennis court, my opponent dominates in the first set. I scrape through the second set to even the score in a tiebreaker. Before we begin the third and final set, the tennis pro unexpectedly stops the match. An hour and a half later, after he has resolved a scheduling conflict, we resume play on a different court where I manage to forge ahead to win.

* * *

Back home with my family in the Boston suburbs, I tackle my mounting responsibilities and dive into a demanding daily routine. Physically active, I jog early in the morning before my children awaken. Away from the classroom for six years, I return to work as a substitute teacher. I attend after-school activities with my children, play tennis, ride horses, volunteer in the community and involve myself in numerous social events. Feverishly energized, I purge, re-organize, and meticulously clean every room in my house. I exist on little sleep and skip meals for days at a time.

Fueling this frenetic existence is an underlying impetus, an irrepressible yearning and inescapable calling to move forward with my spiritual growth. Sheathed in darkness, under the direction of guidance, I travel deeply into realms where spirit invites me to enter. Every night, after I crawl into bed and practice my contemplative exercises, my interior world explodes into colorful dreams, often about preparedness, risk-taking, and persevering through adversity.

Sometimes I dream that I'm both student and teacher in a classroom where I seem to dialogue with my own voice on topics such as unconditional love, surrender, acceptance, and the connection between life experiences and spiritual development. Occasionally I hear violins or a full orchestra playing music or voices speaking in a foreign language.

Intuitively directed to document every episode, I repeatedly awaken to record the details of these inner visions in my journal, dreams that appear to extend beyond the personal. I fill page after page in my spiral notebook with bursts of automatic writing that seem to contain seeds of universal lessons and truths.

As I move through this chaotic chapter in my life I write that I must remain silent, that I must refrain from discussing with anyone this mysterious aspect of my existence. But I also write about my express hope that one day, people across the globe will understand the potential to access their inner knowing, that everyone can listen to their own voice. Love is the key to unlocking this untapped facet of our deeper self.

* * *

On an early morning run I cross the town line where the street changes from pavement to dirt. My senses fill with the sweet fragrance of cotton candy: something feels different. Accustomed to avoiding loose rocks and cavernous potholes on this familiar rural route, I realize that the ground beneath my feet is level and smooth.

In the same instant I hear the rumbling of a noisy engine. When I look up I see a tractor heading in my direction. Attached to the underneath of this earth-moving equipment is a metal blade that scrapes the surface and evens out the bumps in the road.

Forced to jog on the opposite side of the street, I slow down to dodge the obstacles that temporarily hinder my progress. Smiling to myself, I think about the challenges that I faced in the midst of the tennis tournament and the long road that lead to that defining moment. I remind myself that in tennis, whenever I learn a new skill or implement a new strategy, my whole game seems to fall apart. On the verge of a breakthrough, I seem to regress before I'm able to integrate the old with the new and move on to the next level of play.

That night, in a dream, my three children invite me to join them at a special Mass in my hometown at the church where their father and I were married. While my daughters and son wait for me inside my former church, the owner of the bakery shop across the street insists that I park my car inside his store.

As I open the car door, the aroma of freshly baked breads and sweet pastries tempts me, but I resist this temptation and rush outside. Eager to get into the church and reunite with my children, I cross the street and scramble up the front steps of the church, stopping short on the top stair where a crowd blocks the entrance. Determined to get inside, I wriggle through the tight spaces among this cluster of people and find my way into the church.

Walking down the center aisle, looking for my children, I notice a reserved seating area at the front of the church. A wide band of white ribbon cordons off this section of empty pews.

Almost to the altar I hear my younger daughter call to me from the far left side of the church. When I turn around to retrace my footsteps, I notice a renovation, a reconfiguration inside the church. Partway down the center aisle there is now an opening, a pathway where rows of seats have been removed to allow access to the narrow aisles and pews on both sides of the church. In this newly created space, I see a baptismal font.

In the dream, as I walk on this new pathway to join my children, a deafening symphony of inner whirring grips my attention.

Roused by the intensity of this audible vibration I physically awaken, but the resonance echoing through my body and impacting my dream continues to rivet me.

* * *

The following week my husband and I drive to Connecticut to attend a wedding at St. Patrick Church where we were married 17 years before. We park the car, cross the street, and climb the front steps to the entrance of the church. When we get to the top stair, we stop behind a group of wedding guests who wait to be seated.

Once inside I chat with the groomsman who escorts me down the center aisle. Seated with my husband in the front section, I remember the many years that I attended this church with my family. Overflowing with gratitude, I drift into the space that opens when I close my eyes, the interior sanctuary, first discovered when I was a child.

Before the wedding ceremony begins, an electric current sweeps through my body and catapults me from this tranquil state. As the inner whirring rises to an acute level, an irresistible urge compels me to turn around and look behind me. Gazing into the beyond I see the reconfiguration, the pathway on both sides of the center aisle and the baptismal font previously envisioned in my dream.

* * *

Twelve days later, realigned and re-established on solid ground, I resume my spiritual studies. After taking a break from writing in my journal, I once again pick up my pen. Able again to concentrate, I jump back into reading the books left untouched on my nightstand.

Trusting my inner guidance, I close my eyes and open the book that I hold in my hands. I gently rest my fingertips on a page, open my eyes, and silently read the designated passage. I copy this paragraph about transfiguration, a phenomenon in which a person may be allowed to see spiritual realities, into my spiral notebook.

* * *

In 2012, immersed in writing a series of vignettes that trace the events shaping my life, I turn to that journal entry recorded in 1988 and read the passage that I transcribed into my spiral notebook 24 years before. I wonder *why* one might be allowed to witness spiritual realities.

On the computer the next day, I find that one meaning of the word "transfiguration" connotes a complete change into a more spiritual state. As I contemplate this definition, I sense such transfiguration is a life-long process where one may enter into sacred space, see beyond the visible, and open to the mystery of life.

Bumps in the Road

I begin a computer search for the process of transfiguration. Down the list I click on one item, Transfiguration Retreat/Institute of Awakened Mutuality, a program offered at the EarthRise Center at the Institute of Noetic Sciences (IONS). Apollo 14 astronaut Edgar Mitchell founded IONS in 1973.

In November 2010, when I visited the main office of Veriditas in Petaluma, California, I noted its idyllic location on the IONS campus. Sharing the same ground, these two organizations often work together to co-sponsor activities and events that revolve around the labyrinth.

In January 2009, when I first met Reverend Dr. Lauren Artress, founder of Veriditas and the Labyrinth Movement, she asked if I had been to Mystery School. Unfamiliar with this term, I researched Mystery School, now called the Renaissance of Spirit, on the computer. I learned that its founder, Dr. Jean Houston, has held programs and retreats at EarthRise for many years. I also discovered that her mother's maiden name, Todaro, is the same as my paternal grandmother's maiden name.

On the IONS website, I open a link to Jean Houston and play a video in which she promotes the Transfiguration Retreat. Engrossed in her message, I reaffirm my understanding that to see spiritual realities is not meant for any one person. I envision this phenomenon as a catalyst for universal transformation to transcend inequality, advance justice, heal the wounds of humanity and restore integrity and balance in our world.

Cultivate this Gift

Awakening at the brink of dawn, a blue, rectangular light appears on the screen of my inner vision. When I open my eyes I continue to see this illumination, now reflected on the bedroom wall facing me. I concentrate on this geometric figure and deliberately raise and lower my eyes. The image is fluid, moving upward and downward in unison with my focus.

For the next year I'm acutely aware of this interior, blue light and its outward projection onto my bedroom wall, but I don't know why this happens.

* * *

In the fall of 1988, while I privately struggle to resolve my own inner turmoil and cope with the demands of my chaotic life, I devote time to a friend who is suffering through a marital crisis. When I finalize my plans to travel to Atlanta, Georgia, to attend my second worldwide Eckankar seminar, I invite her to come with me, hopeful that she will benefit from this spiritual gathering.

As I inwardly prepare for this annual event I contemplate two pressing concerns. I pray for the strength to endure the rigors of my over-scheduled life, and I ask to connect with a kindred soul. I long to meet someone who, like me, receives intuitive guidance and writes for hours in a private journal.

When I arrive at the seminar in Atlanta, I scan the extensive list of discussion topics and sign up for two specific workshops: *Balancing Your Physical and Spiritual Lives,* and *Why an Eckist Writes.*

The next day, on my way to the first workshop at the convention center, I bump into my friend, Chuck. As we talk I

Cultivate this Gift

tell him about the meeting that I'm going to attend and express my hope that it will address a challenge that I face: how to integrate a frenetic schedule with an all-consuming inner life.

In response, Chuck points out something that I'm not yet able to see for myself. He suggests that *I am* tending to both my daily responsibilities and my inner calling, even though it's often difficult.

Absorbed in conversation, I lose track of time and miss the scheduled workshop on creating balance in our lives, but I realize that I nevertheless received the information that I needed to hear.

That night, at the evening session of the seminar, I briefly slip away from the bustling crowd to find a quiet nook. Sitting on the floor in a walkway, I lean against the wall, close my eyes, and think about the workshop that I plan to attend the next day.

Fifteen minutes later the smell of cigarette smoke bothers me, so I gather my belongings and head to the ladies room. While I stand at a sink, a woman I don't know breezes through the door and stops at the basin next to me. Surprised at the sound of my own voice, I spontaneously explain how I missed a workshop that morning but, while talking with a friend, I learned exactly what I needed to know. I then launch into a description of my writing practice and the bursts of automatic dictation that occur. I also tell her that I've discovered passages in books that seem to echo entries that I've recorded in my own personal journal.

I ask this woman if she knows of anyone whose experiences are similar to mine.

Cultivate this Gift

She exclaims, "Yes. Me! So what is it? Why does it happen?"

I take a deep breath and open to the palpable energy that surges through my body. Aware of my own voice, I do not edit myself and simply express what comes. I tell her that I believe we are all called upon to serve in unique ways. Writing is our gift, a gift that connects us to our source at the center of our being. When we are asked, I go on to say, we must be ready and willing to share with others the truths that reveal themselves to us through inner guidance.

I awaken the next morning resonant with a natural vibration. An inner directive compels me to pick up my pen. Instead of going to the scheduled workshop, a group discussion called *Why an Eckist Writes*, I remain in my hotel room and fill page after page in my spiral notebook.

* * *

Home from Atlanta, I reflect upon my experience at the seminar and remind myself that when I ask for something, it usually comes right away. As I reinforce my understanding that every question I raise sparks an awareness and allows my inner knowing to emerge, and that every answer I receive is a new beginning, an opening into a new question, I wonder: *What's the next step?*

Two weeks later I dream that a friend, the daughter of the real estate agent who found our Cape Cod house, tells me that she knows I want to write a book about my spiritual awakening. Tara, a children's book author, instructs me to contact two people who might be able to assist me.

Cultivate this Gift

Still in the dream, I dial a number that comes to mind automatically. I intently listen to the ringtone until an operator comes on the line. When she informs me that the call cannot be completed, I explain to her why I need help.

The operator tells me that she knows of someone who may be able to assist me. She gives me the telephone number of a local author and wishes me well with my writing.

When I awaken from this dream I feel motivated to take action. Inspired to share my story, I'm hopeful that it might serve as an example to encourage others, that everyone may experience their own spiritual awakening, hear their own Voice.

Hunkered down with a pen and a stack of spiral notebooks, I embark upon my first attempt to write the story of my life.

I enter into this project willingly and open myself to an influx of raw energy that fuels my desire to carry out this life assignment. The deeper I inwardly delve and trust the writing to emerge, the more ferociously I exercise to maintain my sense of equilibrium. Mindful of my tendency to overexert, I write in my journal that I must avoid running my body into the ground.

That winter, while watching a movie with my husband and our next-door neighbors, the wife, Margot, my running partner, asks in a whisper if I will receive remuneration for writing this book.

I answer "no," that I don't expect to be paid for taking on this task, but I know it's something I must do.

Throughout the spring, as I diligently work on writing this book, I continue to see the rectangular, blue light that first

Cultivate this Gift

appeared in my inner and outer vision one year earlier. Without knowing why, this image comforts me and keeps me focused on my writing.

During the summer, after months of pouring my heart into this project, I reach an impasse in my effort to eke out the narrative. I realize that although I've written volumes about my dreams and life experiences, my compilation of writings merely tells the beginning of a story that does not yet have a middle or an end.

Unable to unlock the secrets that I keep hidden deep inside of me, I realize that I'm not yet ready to finish the work that I've started. Frustrated by my inability to access the missing pieces that I need to move forward, I push my body beyond its breaking point.

That fall, in constant pain and unable to walk, I make an appointment to see an orthopedic surgeon. The doctor tells me that I have a bulging disc in my back that is pinching a nerve. He prescribes anti-inflammatory drugs and orders me to rest in bed for one month before starting physical therapy. At first I think that he's joking about staying in bed for a month, but my heart sinks when I realize that he's dead serious.

On the fourth day of my confinement, I close my eyes and focus on the recurring, blue light that comforts me. In stillness I observe this familiar image dramatically change before my eyes. As the blueness of the rectangle darkens into blackness, a glowing arc of brilliant, white light surrounds the geometric form and attaches to all four sides. At that precise moment, tongues of fire, streaks of dazzling flames, shoot outward from the periphery.

When I open my eyes I continue to see the projection of this transformed vision on my bedroom wall. Playfully I raise my eyes up to the ceiling and back down on the wall. I watch as the image moves up and down accordingly.

Sensing this may be a sign for me to resume writing, I decide to try a different approach to my narrative. On my second attempt to tell my story, I bridge each personal experience with a universal awareness. I begin by stating my purpose for writing this book and branch into my observation that children experience their physical and spiritual lives as one and the same.

While I work on this reclaimed project, one month of bed rest stretches into four. In May 1990, on my son's eighth birthday, I undergo my first back surgery, but the operation fails to remedy the problem. Six weeks later I still can't walk. When I consult with the head of neurosurgery at a Boston hospital, he tells me that unless I have a second surgery, I will be crippled for the rest of my life.

During the stretch of time between my two surgeries, while I am confined to bed rest, the inner vision morphs once again. As the interior fabric of the geometric figure softens, the streaks of brilliant white light transform into flames of gold. Now three-dimensional, the image vertically divides into two halves. As I focus on this new configuration, I clearly see that this illumination is an open book.

Cultivate this Gift

I interpret this event as a sign to continue working on the book that I have now twice begun to write. Prompted to launch my third attempt, I open a pad of green, legal-sized paper and draft an outline. I sort my previous writings into six categories: chronology, dreams, outer experiences, personal growth, direct perceptions and letters.

In August 1990, on my husband's and my nineteenth wedding anniversary, I undergo a second back surgery followed by two and a half years of physical therapy to regain the ability to walk independently. Throughout this time I continue with my writing, but the book that I envision remains a work in progress.

For inspiration I turn to a journal entry that I recorded three years earlier and contemplate the words that came to me through guidance.

The day will come when the words you write will serve a purpose. The stories you tell will convey a message. This writing is not only for you; it's for everyone on the path. Cultivate this gift for the benefit of mankind to help others come to know the love that abounds.

Resonating with this voice, an expression of my own Truth, the intuitive knowing that springs from the divine, my body pulsates with a dynamic energy that erupts from center. Compelled to release the explosive internal pressure, I reach for my pen.

The writing is part of the service that you have been called upon to do. The right time will come for all the words to be organized, clarified, and set down in a manner that will be useful to all who will read them.

Cultivate this Gift

The use of the language is an essential tool in the dispersal of information. Have greater confidence in your ability to use the appropriate words to facilitate your mission. Take advantage of every opportunity to allow Spirit to work with you and through you.

Reach deep into your heart and search for those descriptive words that will most clearly convey your message. You will be able to universally convey the spiritual knowledge that you have gained on every level only when you have acquired the skills to verbally communicate this knowledge on a personal level. When you are able to express your deepest awarenesses in a way that can be understood, you will then be better prepared to assume the greater responsibility of communicating the love of God, through you, to all waiting Souls.

* * *

Today, as this story unfolds, the words that echoed through my body 24 years ago seem to hold true in the present as the aforementioned dream foretold: an invisible "operator" leads me to a local author who might be able to help me write a book.

In 2008, after I discover the missing link, the key information that ties past to present and allows me to finish this story, a female minister at a Congregational Church in West Hartford, Connecticut, provides me with the names of two women with whom I might speak about my spiritual awakening. I reach out to both and hear back from one, Reverend Dr. Lauren Artress, an Episcopal priest in San Francisco, who directs me to Catharine Clarke, my writing coach and editor.

Julie

In December 1992, when my son is in fifth grade, one of his classmates is diagnosed with Ewing's Sarcoma, a rare form of bone cancer that typically strikes children and adolescents. Two weeks later the elementary school principal calls to ask if I am available to tutor this child. Her mother is one of my closest friends.

Julie, a bright and multi-talented ten-year-old, enjoys ballet, singing, reading, and poetry. A collector of sea glass and foreign currency, she especially loves to walk on the beach, play with her dog, Sweetie, and spend time with her family and friends.

Over the next three years Julie undergoes multiple surgeries, endures the grueling side effects of chemotherapy, and receives a bone marrow transplant. Although she is frequently homebound or hospitalized, she maintains a close relationship with a wide circle of supportive friends.

On good days when she is able to attend school or enjoy an outing with family or friends, Julie selects a fashionable hat from her wardrobe, well suited for each special occasion. Fun-loving and sociable, she inspires everyone she meets with her infectious smile and her appetite for life.

On a flexible schedule that accommodates her daily needs, Julie and I cover lessons in math, reading, writing, social studies and science. Beyond their educational value,

Julie

these tutorial sessions create fertile ground for cultivating our trusting friendship.

In the midst of one session Julie asks why I limp and walk with a cane. After I explain that I had two back surgeries to repair a bulging disc in my spine, she talks about the cancer that is in her spine. During this poignant exchange, Julie confides that she feels badly for all the children in the hospital who have cancer, especially those who are sicker than she is.

When I arrive at Julie's house one afternoon, I quickly realize that she is not up for an academic lesson. Her heart is willing, but the lingering effect of her medications makes it impossible for her to concentrate on her schoolwork. As a diversion, I pick up a deck of cards that lay on the coffee table in the family room. While shuffling, I playfully ask Julie if she'd like to see a card trick.

As her eyes follow my every move, I divide the cards into several piles and place them on the coffee table. I ask her to select three of the piles and to turn over the top card of two. After shuffling the remaining cards, I call out the card that lays face down on top of the third pile.

On that day I teach Julie the card trick that my older cousin taught me when I was a child. Still a mystery to me, I can't explain how or why it works, but like Julie, I'm thrilled every time it does.

When Julie is admitted to the hospital, I drive to Boston with two of my closest friends to visit with her.

Julie

Along with Julie's mother, we four steadfast friends gather together with our families every year on Christmas Eve to celebrate the holiday, a long-lasting tradition that began before Julie became ill and that endures to this day.

In May 1995, when my older daughter is a senior, Julie asks me what it feels like to be a student in high school. Perceptive beyond her 13 years, she tells me that she knows she won't live to graduate with her classmates. She asks if she may come with our family to our daughter's high school graduation.

A half-hour before we leave, Julie's mother brings her to our house so she can see the graduate dressed in her cap and gown. That night Julie musters the strength to sit through the entire ceremony, but she is too tired to come back to our house for the party afterward. In the car on the way home, she thanks us for taking her to graduation and tells us that she will always remember this day.

Six months later, on the day after Christmas, Julie takes her final breath on this earth. Beyond our deep sadness she leaves all of us a precious gift, a permanent imprint of her courage, wisdom, compassion, and kindness.

* * *

The mother of three teen-agers, I pour all of my energy into living my everyday life. I leave Eckankar, the spiritual path that I had followed after separating from the Catholic Church. I give up the daily practice of contemplative exercises. I no longer record my innermost thoughts or

Julie

nightly dreams in a personal journal. I stop working on the book that I had envisioned, a story about the events that have shaped my life.

At a crossroad, I pack all 17 spiral notebooks containing my private journal entries into a sturdy shopping bag, as well as stacks of legal-sized notepads and computer printouts that document my attempts to write a book. I stash this oversized bag in the back corner of my bedroom closet, where my secreted writings lay dormant for the next ten years.

* * *

Employed in a neighboring town as a tutor for students with special needs, I work with children in public schools, private homes and hospitals. The following year I accept a position as a special education instructional assistant in a middle school and enroll in a graduate program to earn a Master of Education in Special Education. A veteran teacher, I did not originally seek out this field, but answering the call to be Julie's tutor led to my new vocation.

The New Millennium

On family vacation at the 1996 Summer Olympics in Atlanta, Georgia, I plunk down on a bench in Centennial Olympic Park and wait for the live concert to begin. When the music starts my husband and children join me at this bench, our designated meeting place. At the end of the riveting performance country singers Tim McGraw and Faith Hill, now husband and wife, share a kiss on stage.

The next day we drive to Birmingham, Alabama, the venue for the women's soccer games. We have tickets for an upcoming match between the United States and China.

When we arrive at the stadium the following morning we learn that during the night, a bomb exploded in Centennial Olympic Park. One woman was killed and 111 people were injured in this attack. Later that day we realize that this deadly bomb had been planted next to the bench where my family and I had gathered the night before to watch the concert.

On the spacious grounds of this celebrated park, the Quilt of Remembrance, a mosaic of stones from around the world, pays tribute to the victims of this horrific crime. Here an eternal light shines in memory of Alice Hawthorne, the woman who died there.

* * *

On the evening of December 31, 1999, my family and I board a return flight from Orlando to Boston. We are

The New Millennium

midair at the stroke of midnight when we enter into the new millennium, the year 2000.

Soon after, early one January morning, my younger daughter and I drive the hour toward our beach house on the Cape. Observing a family tradition, we crack open the car windows to inhale the salt air as we cross the Sagamore Bridge.

Fifteen minutes later, just three miles from our house, my cell phone rings. My husband, a seasoned traveler, tells me that he didn't get on his scheduled flight to Chicago because something is wrong with his vision. He says that he can barely see.

My daughter and I reverse direction, drive back over the bridge, and head toward home, back to the Boston suburbs. Hurrying along the highway, my cell phone rings again.

In the Emergency Room at Newton-Wellesley Hospital, my husband has been diagnosed with bleeding ulcers and transported to the Intensive Care Unit.

By the third day of his hospitalization, his condition appears stable. That evening I kiss my husband goodnight, drive home from the hospital, and crawl into bed. As I reach to turn off the light, the phone rings. Startled, I glance at the clock. It's 11:45 pm.

On the phone I hear the doctor say, "Your husband is in trouble. He has a serious re-bleed. You need to get here right away."

The New Millennium

Propped on the edge of the bed I ask if my husband might die.

The doctor answers, "Yes."

As shockwaves convulse my body I call Margot, my dear friend and next-door neighbor. Within minutes I hear her car pull into our driveway.

In his hospital room a flurry of activity surrounds my husband. I stand at his bedside while Margot, a hematologist, discreetly assesses the medical emergency. His doctor, a colleague of Margot's husband, hands her the laboratory reports. As the staff whisks my husband to the operating room I hear the doctor say that the procedure to stop his internal bleeding will take less than an hour.

Margot offers to stay with me at the hospital, but I insist that she go home and get some sleep. Three hours later I learn that complications arose during the surgery. Alone in the waiting room, I pray that my husband will survive his ordeal.

Another hour passes before a nurse comes to tell me that my husband will soon be out of surgery. When I see him in the Recovery Room, I hardly recognize him.

The following week he is discharged from the hospital. On a strict dietary regimen he gradually regains his strength. After a three-month-long recuperation, he eases back to work.

* * *

The New Millennium

My Uncle Joe, a decorated World War II veteran, lives in our hometown with his 97-year-old mother, my maternal grandmother. He never talks about his experiences in the war, but I know that he fought in five invasions in Africa and Italy, including the Battle of Anzio in 1944, and that he narrowly survived the sinking of a ship.

One day, while sitting with my grandmother in her living room, I hear my uncle moaning in his bedroom. On my way upstairs to check on him I hear him cry out, "I wish I had died in the war."

That afternoon I call his doctor, who prescribes an antidepressant to help my uncle cope with the invisible scars of a war that ended more than five decades before.

I remember that my mother had told me when I was a child that my Uncle Joe had been a self-taught artist and an accomplished stonemason but had abandoned these crafts when he returned home from the war. A skilled tradesman, he opened a shoe repair shop that remained in business throughout the 1950s. To this day I associate the distinctive smell of leather and shoe polish with my Uncle Joe.

* * *

One Sunday when I'm ten years old, while playing cards after family dinner in my parent's kitchen, I tell my Uncle Joe that I can't draw and then explain what happened in my fifth grade classroom.

The New Millennium

Sitting at my desk I watch the art teacher, Mrs. Wilcox, draw a picture of a Native American on a piece of construction paper that she has taped to the blackboard. Following her directions, I pick up my crayons and try my best to duplicate her artwork while she patrols the classroom and inspects each student's progress. When her footsteps behind me fall silent, I keep my eyes glued to my desk. Engulfed in her shadow I hear her criticize, "Your Indian doesn't look like my Indian."

Without saying a word my Uncle Joe picks up a pencil, opens to a clean page in the pad that we're using to keep score for our card game, and shows me how to sketch two subjects: a human profile and a galloping horse. This is the only time in my life that I see my uncle demonstrate his artistic talent.

The following year on my eleventh birthday my uncle surprises me with a paint-by-number set. Working with a fine-tipped brush and an array of paint-filled glass vials, I spend an entire summer on this ambitious project. When I finish the step-by-step rendition of Leonardo da Vinci's *The Last Supper*, my parents hang the framed picture on the wall in our kitchen.

One year later, on my twelfth birthday, my Uncle Joe presents me with a massive book entitled *Leonardo da Vinci*. He tells me that I will find everything that I need to know about life in this book.

The New Millennium

In the spring of 2000, my 78-year-old Uncle Joe suffers abdominal pain and is admitted to Johnson Memorial Hospital in Stafford Springs, Connecticut, where both of my parents died. When he is discharged from the hospital he's transported to a nursing home for specialized care.

One day, while visiting with him, I notice that my uncle is particularly interested in hearing about my children. After listening to an update on the lives of his grandnephew and grandnieces, now in high school and college, my uncle articulates his one request. He asks me to tell all three of my children that he loves them.

That afternoon, when I say goodbye to my Uncle Joe, I'm unaware that this conversation will be our last.

At my grandmother's house I remove my uncle's clothing and personal belongings from his bedroom. In the top drawer of his maple dresser I find his black, leather wallet. Bulging with family photographs, the wallet contains worn-out pictures of my grandmother, my grandfather, my mother, and my Uncle Mike in his Navy uniform, all taken in the 1940s; elementary school pictures of my sister and me from the 1950s; school photos of my children in the 1980s and a 1983 family snapshot of my husband and me with our children when they were one, three, and five years old.

My quiet reverie abruptly ends when my grandmother calls out from downstairs, "Joey, where are you?"

The New Millennium

In the living room I sit on the round, brown-leather hassock next to my grandmother's blue recliner. As I reach for her hand, I again tell her that Joe is not here.

Afflicted with dementia, she seems unable to comprehend that her son, my Uncle Joe, is dead. She tells me that he will soon be home. Rooted in the past, my grandmother then confuses me with my deceased mother. She calls me Mary and asks why I'm not at work.

Inundated with poignant memories, I raise my eyes and focus on the two pictures that hang on the wall over my grandmother's couch. Prominently displayed in her living room for 60 years, these oil paintings are the only remaining evidence of my Uncle Joe's artistry. Both works, a cozy cottage set in winter and a bent tree on the edge of a cliff, now hang in my home on Cape Cod.

While writing this chapter of my life story, I retrieve the oversized book, *Leonardo da Vinci*, from my basement, the gift that my Uncle Joe gave me 50 years ago on my twelfth birthday. As I skim some of the text and browse through the pictures, I recall reading that in his lifetime, some 500 years earlier, Leonardo da Vinci was a Freemason.

My thoughts instantly turn to the Masonic symbol, the angular metal object with the letter "G" in the center, that I discovered 26 years ago in the basement of our old beach house. I have since learned that this sign, composed of a mathematical compass and a square,

The New Millennium

relates to the sacred geometry that sometimes forms the basis of a labyrinth's pattern.

Reflecting upon the Masonic practice of discalceation, a ritual in which initiates remove one of their shoes, I think about the men and women in some religious orders who are discalced, or barefooted. I'm reminded that as a child who enjoyed being barefoot, I often found a way around my father's request that I wear shoes outside.

Musing, I note that the root of my father's surname and the root of the word "discalced" are the same. I remember my aunt, one of my father's sisters, telling me that our family name, Maniscalchi, translated as two words, hand and shoe, means "maker of shoes." Years later, on a trip to Disney World with my husband and children, I look up my maiden name at a genealogical shop in EPCOT and confirm that Maniscalchi means shoemaker, the occupation of my Italian ancestry.

As I sit at my dining room table to write this vignette, I gaze at the garden labyrinth that graces my front yard. Awakened to the circuitous path that dwells within, I envision the shoe repair shop that my Uncle Joe ran when I was a child. I recall that my father's brother, my recently deceased Uncle Chic, once lived with his wife and children on Shoemaker Lane. I remember that after my children were born, my mother worked as a bookkeeper for Vincent's Family Shoes, a store in our hometown that has served five generations. And as I look beyond the sliding

The New Millennium

glasss doors into the backyard of my home on the Cape, I revel in the ebb and flow of the ever-changing, tidal water in Shoestring Bay.

* * *

In November 2000, on the day after Thanksgiving at our house in the Boston suburbs, our next-door neighbors – Margot, her husband, and their three children – along with Margot's sister – feast with our family on leftover turkey with all the trimmings. At this fun-filled gathering I notice a change in Margot's naturally slender body. It seems to me that her trim waistline and flat stomach have expanded.

At that moment my dear friend turns to me and says, "I feel fat. I have to stop eating so much."

One month later Margot, a specialist in hematology, an expert in blood banking and transfusion medicine, and a professor of pathology at Harvard Medical School, abruptly returns home from a medical meeting in Florida. Bloated, fatigued, and suffering from abdominal pain, she meets with her internist and soon after is admitted to the hospital.

After she rebounds from her initial surgery and her first round of chemotherapy, Margot talks to me about the isolation and fear that accompany her diagnosis. Cautiously optimistic that her cancer could go into remission, she confides that even if it does, she will wake up every morning wondering if today is the day that her disease will return. She then tells me that she wants to write a book about living with ovarian cancer, a pragmatic guide that may be useful to both doctors and patients.

A quintessential academic, Margot enrolls in a creative writing course at Harvard Extension School and compiles a series of essays about her illness and its profound impact upon her identity. In her revealing narrative, *The Glass Room*, Margot writes, "…the fabric of my life was torn and time itself was unraveling."

In the fall of 2003 Margot undergoes a bone marrow transplant at M. D. Anderson Cancer Center in Houston, Texas. In an ironic twist of fate she is now the recipient of advances in medical research and technology that she pioneered and championed in her field of expertise.

While in Houston with Margot for six weeks of her 12-week ordeal, I attend a two-day class at the hospital to qualify as her caregiver. Under nursing supervision I learn to perform specific tasks such as flushing her surgically implanted central line and changing her sterile bandages.

One night, engrossed in conversation while sitting in the living room of a temporary rental apartment, Margot and I share our most significant lifelong memories and our deepest personal secrets. During this intimate exchange I tell her about the family crisis that erupted 35 years before when my mother and my sister concealed the truth about the baby that my sister abandoned. I describe the agony of withholding this information from my father because my mother threatened to never forgive me if I ever told him the truth. I explain how my Uncle Mike, the older of my mother's two brothers, wrongly blamed me for causing her unhappiness. I sum up what I've shard by confiding in Margot that in the past, false accusations have triggered my bouts with severe depression.

She responds, "I've never met anyone like you. You took care of your uncle in your own home when he was ill. I don't understand how you can be so kind to the people who have hurt you so much."

Past her bedtime, Margot gets up from the couch and asks, "How do you survive on so little sleep?"

Hospitalized for weeks, Margot expresses her concern that I will be exhausted if I continue to spend every waking hour at her bedside. Insistent that I take occasional breaks, she chooses excursions for me to enjoy. One afternoon, on an historical tour of the city, I discover Houston's underground tunnel system. On other outings I visit the Museum of Fine Arts and explore the campus at Rice University. And in the Butterfly Garden at the Museum of Natural Science, I watch dozens of winged insects hatch out of their cocoons and begin a new way of life.

On the first of November, the day that the Catholic Church celebrates All Saints Day, Margot, an accomplished quilter, asks me to go to the International Quilting Festival, an annual event, and to take lots of pictures of the amazing variety of quilts on display. When I arrive at this vast exhibit I realize that 16 years earlier, in the fall of

The New Millennium

1987, I attended my first Worldwide Eckankar seminar at this same venue, the Houston Convention Center. Filled with vivid memories of that major spiritual gathering and pivotal event in my life, I walk for hours among thousands of unique quilts as each whispers to me its own life story.

Keep Writing

When my husband and children arrive at our beach house on Cape Cod, our younger daughter calls me on the phone and says, "Mom, this is so hard. I wish we were all together as a family."

* * *

Several times a day I walk down the long driveway beside my house in the Boston suburbs to see Margot, my dear friend and next-door neighbor. Each time I enter her family room, now her first-floor bedroom, I greet her with a smile. One of her nurses, a family friend, has taught me how to tend to the intravenous lines and stomach drains that are part of her daily medical regimen. Nearing the end of her battle with ovarian cancer, Margot is in hospice care.

On this sunlit morning a peaceful stillness greets me when I open the front door and step inside Margot's house. Realizing that her husband and children are not yet up, I tiptoe across the foyer and into the bedroom to check on her. Assured that she is comfortably asleep in her hospital bed, I return home.

In my kitchen I sit at the round, oak table with two of Margot's friends who stayed overnight at my house. As I look through the bay window and into my backyard, I remember Margot saying that she would like her friends to fill the new planter on her back deck with colorful flowers. One friend, the woman whose husband built the large, wooden planter for Margot, says that she will get the flowers.

Focused on Margot's request, I feel a blast of energy surge through my body. I'm aware of an inner whirring, an interior vibration that rises to an earsplitting decibel. In this instant I instinctively know that I may not turn back. I must allow myself to go wherever this current leads me.

Ten years prior a climactic event such as this would have compelled me to reach for my pen. Now, instead of writing in a private journal, I vocally expel the explosive pressure that wells up inside of me.

From the depths of my being I scream, "Margot is *translated*."

Subliminally aware that Margot's two friends are present, I nevertheless cross a threshold where the floodgates to my inner self burst wide open. I am subject to the ultimate heartbreak, the indescribable pain and cumulative suffering of all creation.

While suspended in this excruciating state I somehow feel internally fortified. I intuitively understand that my wailing is a primordial release, a hopeful plea for healing, harmony, equality, and justice for all of humanity. In this moment I recognize my own voice as an instrument, a conduit that may give voice to the silent, a catalyst that may stimulate individual growth and universal transformation.

In union with One and All, I resonate again with my grandmother's words, "Nothing new ever happens in this world. People have the same experiences over and over again."

Keep Writing

In this awakened state, as I imagine the existence of someone I'm yet to meet, someone whose inner world is akin to mine, I hear an interior voice declare, *Whatever you need will be provided.*

Soon after, Margot's two friends gather their belongings and head next door to stay at her house.

While resting on the couch in my living room, scenes from my childhood come into view. I am the youngster who emerged unharmed after falling underneath a moving 18-wheel, tractor-trailer truck. I am the ten-year old who longed to take on all of her father's pain when he was ill, the girl who secretly asked to die so he could live.

In stillness I ponder the meaning of my spontaneous cry, "Margot is *translated*." I guardedly consider that this word choice may imply a certain spiritual state: conveyed to heaven without death.

An hour later I walk down the long driveway to see Margot. The moment I enter her bedroom she worriedly asks, "How are you feeling?"

I explain that it may have appeared to her friends that I was breaking down, but, from within, the experience was a purifying and strengthening revelation. I tell her that I feel rejuvenated.

Margot then tells me that something unusual happened to her earlier in the morning. Frail and emaciated, she describes how she woke up feeling refreshed and talkative. She whispers, "I had so much energy – and you *missed* it."

Keep Writing

* * *

In the wee hours of the following morning an overwhelming urge awakens me. I climb out of bed, walk down the stairs, and turn on a light in the basement. In the workshop I dig through an old cardboard box and pull out a blank spiral notebook.

Sitting at the kitchen table I peer into the darkness that blankets the bay window. I feel my heart pound in my chest as the intensity of the inner whirring increases exponentially. Following inner guidance, I reach for my pen and resume the lifesaving practice that I had abandoned ten years prior.

With unparalleled clarity I fill page after page in the spiral notebook. Four hours later, when the upsurge subsides, I turn back to the beginning and read the detailed writings that have emerged.

Reconnected with my innermost Self, I walk upstairs to my bedroom, open my closet door, and pull out the large shopping bag where I had stashed away my writing notebooks ten years before, after Julie, a child dear to my heart, died of cancer. On top of the heaping pile of old writings in the shopping bag, I add the latest spiral notebook. I carry the heavy paper sack down to the garage and load my life's work into my car.

After packing an overnight bag I pay a visit to Margot. The instant she sees me she asks, "Why aren't you on the Cape with your family?"

Keep Writing

I explain that until now, I wasn't ready to leave.

With knowing eyes she looks at me and says, "You are my best friend. I wish I had spent more time with you."

* * *

When I arrive at our beach house my husband, our children, and three of their closest friends come outside to greet me. Anxious to learn how Margot is feeling, they sit with me on the front porch to talk.

Later that day, longtime friends, a married couple, stop by for a visit. When they ask about Margot, the intimate conversation that ensues opens an avenue, a safe passageway. I tell them about the emotional release that occurred at my kitchen table. I show them the shopping bag filled with spiral notebooks, legal-sized notepads, and computer printouts that document my attempts to write a book. I pick up the spiral notebook from the top of this heaping pile and read aloud the detailed writings that have most recently emerged.

I share with my friends that I believe we are all on the same spiritual path, and that through the practice of writing, I hope to one day discover a universal language that will help people to find their way.

Processing the whole story, the husband asks if I know of anyone who has had the same kinds of experiences that I've had. He then points to the shopping bag and inquires, "Have you shared these writings with anyone else?"

Keep Writing

I feel my heart pound in my chest as I answer, "Yes, my childhood friend, Chuck."

* * *

On the eve of the Fourth of July holiday, when our younger daughter invites her closest friends to our house, one of her roommates asks if she may call a few more people to come over.

When my husband and I return home after dining out, we pull into our driveway and see a crowd gathered around a fire in our backyard. Our daughter explains that there are more people here than she'd expected because one young man, whom her roommate called, had asked for permission to bring along his ten houseguests.

Cordial and respectful, each of the young adults greets my husband and me to say hello. Some we have known for years, but most are visitors who we are meeting for the first time.

On this tranquil summer evening I have no inkling that one year from now, this impromptu gathering, a momentary reprieve from the overwhelming sadness of Margot's rapid decline, will give rise to false accusations that, for me, trigger a major depression.

* * *

The following morning, while my family attends the Fourth of July parade in our quaint village, I settle into a quiet space in our beach house to contemplate. When I finish writing in my private journal I go upstairs to my bedroom, open my bureau drawer, and pull out an old tee shirt printed with the expression, "Experience the joy of living."

On my way to the beach I pass by the Greek revival home that Margot and her husband had sold several years before. As I inhale the salt air and watch the sunlight dance on the surface of the water, I notice an airplane overhead towing a banner that says, "Experience the Excellence." While strolling barefoot on the sand I notice a child wearing a tee shirt with a picture of a heart, an EKG strip, and a saying that reads, "…and the beat goes on." Each of these sightings fills me with a sense of peace, hope, and unity.

That night my husband and I spend a quiet evening at home. This year's holiday marks the end of a 19-year tradition of co-hosting an annual cookout for family and friends in celebration of Independence Day.

The next morning I load the heavy shopping bag filled with my collective writings into my car and drive back to our home in the Boston suburbs. When I pull into the garage, I grab one spiral notebook and walk down the long driveway to see Margot.

The Dark Shadow

In the spring of 2006, while dining with friends at an Italian restaurant, I enter a nightmare when one woman blurts out, "Your daughter had a Fourth of July party last year and didn't invite my children."

* * *

Three months later, at a bridal luncheon for my older daughter, this friend arrives late and leaves abruptly. Someone tells me that she's not feeling well.

That afternoon I call her to ask if she's feeling any better. When she says, "No," I walk over to her house to check on her.

Standing on the step outside her front door, I find that she's not sick at all. She's upset because she claims that at the shower, her daughter was not invited to sit at my daughter's table. When I explain that no guest's seat was pre-arranged, she nonetheless alleges that her daughter was shunned. She accuses me of gossiping that one of my children's friends had been mean to her daughter when they were ten years old, well over a decade and a half earlier.

During this odd conversation I learn that my neighbor's lifelong friend, a woman with whom she's had a falling out, saw her walking in the rain and gave her a ride home from the bridal shower. When I suggest that this may be an opening to put her ill feelings behind her and forgive her old friend, she says, "Never."

The Dark Shadow

When I get home my daughter asks how our neighbor is doing. I say that I'm not sure. Concerned that she is seriously ill, my daughter asks if she is dying. The moment I assure her that the woman is not sick but upset, and tell her the story, my daughter insists upon talking to her in person.

A half hour later she returns home looking pale and confused. She tells me that when she apologized for the misunderstanding and said that she would never do anything to hurt her daughter, the woman accused her of excluding her children from the aforementioned Fourth of July gathering.

Distraught, my daughter says, "Mom, I didn't invite anyone to that party. I have to stay positive. I don't know why she is blaming me for something that I didn't do."

At a family meeting with my husband and our three children, we consider that the woman's demeanor likely points to an underlying issue that has nothing to do with us. We decide to disregard her false accusations and put this matter to rest.

But something dark churns deep inside of me. I miss my dear friend Margot who died ten months earlier. Four months after her death, our close friends lost their 22-year-old son to cancer. And only ten weeks after his passing, my brother-in-law died at home while watching a movie with my sister, just five days shy of his fifty-fifth birthday.

* * *

The Dark Shadow

That fall, three months after our daughter's wedding, my neighbor comes to my house to talk. During this conversation I again explain that the year before's impromptu Fourth of July gathering was not a planned event. She says that she's sorry if she hurt me, but insists that her children were intentionally excluded from that Fourth of July party.

Realizing that she is in pain, I try to help her see that oftentimes blaming others is an attempt to relieve our own emotional suffering when we may be searching for answers. I suggest that she look inside herself to uncover the real source of her heartache.

Unable to reach her, I feel the energy drain from my body. I listen to my voice as I say aloud the words that come to me from inner guidance. I tell her that I can't allow her negativity to affect me, and that I must not take her accusations personally. But, I'm powerless to heed my own advice.

* * *

In December a friend who shares my avid interest in real estate emails a listing for a house that's for sale on the Cape. In March 2007, after selling our home in the Boston suburbs and our beach house, my husband and I move into a home on Shoestring Bay. We buy a second home in Connecticut where his office is located.

In spite of these major changes, I can't escape from the dark shadow that follows me. I feel responsible for my

The Dark Shadow

daughter's victimization on the day of her bridal shower. This triggers an old, dire response, because I identify with the wound of being falsely accused and its subsequent suffering. I berate myself for failing to help my friend see the truth. Over and over again I hear inside my head: *Mom, I didn't invite anyone to that party. I have to stay positive. I don't know why she is blaming me for something that I didn't do.*

In the grip of severe depression, an unsettling family matter sends me over the edge. I feel at odds with my son's girlfriend. Blurry-eyed, I can barely see the road through my tears as the speedometer in my car approaches 100 miles per hour.

Just one sharp turn and the pain will be over.

* * *

Shattering the delusion that I'm able to hide my illness from my children, my son spends three days with me on the Cape. When he gives me the name of a clinical psychologist who specializes in treating patients with depression, I explain that in the past, these bouts have lasted two years. *If I can just get through the next six months, I'll be okay*, I tell him.

In my first session with the therapist I tell her that for me to heal, I've got to get back to my daily contemplative practice of prayerful writing, but I don't know how. When I talk to her about my recent, heartbreaking losses and explain how a friend's false accusations and unbridled negativity have triggered my depression, she advises me to sever all ties with that friend and to simplify my life so that my relationships and my surroundings reflect my true self.

The second time we meet I reveal my family's hidden story. I tell her about the baby that my sister abandoned 40 years ago. I talk about how my mother insisted that I conceal the truth about the baby from my father, and how this anguished me. Finally, I explain how my uncle wrongly blamed me for my mother's unhappiness; though I sensed it was the result of her own deception and betrayal.

On the third visit I divulge the details of my own secret inner life. I tell her about my interior connection with Chuck, my childhood friend, and disclose the mysterious events that have occurred in my life. I describe the painting that Chuck unveiled, a visual representation of a scene that I had previously imagined. I confide that I have twice heard a thunderous voice: first, *Trust in God and no one else*, and two years later, *Your patience is rewarded*.

During the fourth session I talk about my extensive writings, the detailed journal entries from years ago, and my attempts to write a book that I've envisioned. I describe the recurring rectangular, blue light that 18 years before morphed into a golden, open book.

When I speak to the psychologist about unconditional love, unity, and Oneness in being, she asks, first, if I believe in reincarnation, and then, if I know about Saint Teresa. I tell her that Teresa, without an "h," is my confirmation name.

The Dark Shadow

Online I research Teresa of Ávila. I learn that she is the patron saint of headache sufferers. Her symbols are a heart, an arrow, and a book. Along with John of the Cross, she is the founder of the Discalced Carmelites, a "shoeless" religious order. I read:

...migraine headaches...a pierced heart...a book......my confirmation name: Teresa......my maiden name: Maniscalchi...discalced...

Mustering all of my courage, I continue my computer search.

...her mother asked her to keep a secret from her father... caught in the middle...blamed for things she didn't do...hid her depression...struggled to reconcile her physical life with her spiritual life...plagued with self-doubt...a sole confidant...couldn't walk for three years...mystical experiences...for a time she stopped praying... wrote in seclusion...twice heard a voice...spiritual marriage...the garden...outgoing...prayed to learn how to be of service...faced her fears...patient...loved nature...gave up certain friends... reluctantly joined a choir...interested in real estate...brother-in-law died suddenly...nursed a sick friend...

At times in her life Teresa wanted to die, first for the love of her father and then because she thought she had served her purpose for living....

She read passages in books that seemed to describe her life....

Nearing 60, she set out to accomplish her most important work....

* * *

Three weeks later, at our fifth meeting, I thank the therapist for helping me to move forward with my recovery.

The Dark Shadow

She responds, "The moment I heard your voice I felt the love. I knew that you were stuck and needed help to get unstuck."

At this final session I share information that I've discovered when researching Teresa of Ávila online. After thoughtful consideration, the therapist says, "Now you have what you need to finish your story."

* * *

In memory of Margot, our younger daughter twice runs the Boston Marathon in support of Dana-Farber Cancer Institute. On April 15, 2013, minutes from completing the celebrated 26.2-mile footrace, she is rerouted off-course to a secure location after two devastating bombs explode at the finish line. In April the following year, on Patriot's Day, she runs her third Boston Marathon and safely crosses the legendary finish line on Boylston Street.

In August 2014, nine years after Margot's death, while recovering from bilateral pulmonary emboli (blood clots in my lungs), my diagnosis of chronic lymphocytic leukemia (CLL), a slow-growing cancer of the blood, is confirmed. In this ironic twist, as a patient with cancer, I return to Boston, to the hematological world that once was Margot's professional domain.

Synchronicity

In the car on my way to visit my college roommate, I turn the corner of my street. For the first time in two years I hear the inner whirring, the interior vibration that connects me with center and the true source of my aliveness.

* * *

In the spring of 2008, I begin a yearlong ambitious project. While organizing, rewriting, and transcribing on computer hundreds of pages of handwritten journal entries from spiral notebooks, I come upon a dream that I had on October 30, 1990.

In this dream my lifelong friend, Chuck, sits in a large, overstuffed chair in the living room of an old house. I sit on the floor and rest my back on his shins. We greet several people as they file in and out of the house.

Chuck, an artist, says, "Come to the studio with me. There's something I have to show you. We're going to look at a painting."

In the studio I busy myself with simple tasks. I hang up coats. I help children put on their mittens. Then I walk into a nearby room and rearrange pieces of sculpture that are on display.

Chuck patiently waits for me. When I return to the studio he says, "Look at this painting and tell me what you see."

I describe the circle of fresh flowers in one part of the painting.

He says, "No. That's not it. I don't want to talk about purity or the Virgin Mary."

I point out the contrasting intensity of colors and explain how the painting draws you in and pushes you back at the same time.

Again he says, "No. That's not it. What do you see?"

I avoid looking at the pile of discarded sunglasses in the bottom left corner of the painting. Chuck stands by me and insists that I tell him what I see.

In the dream I finally admit that I have to stop hiding behind the dark shades. I have to take off one more pair of blinders and add them to the pile. I see that it's time to step out of the darkness and allow the light of truth to shine, no matter how hard it may be to look at its brilliance.

* * *

In June 2008, I drive to New York City with two close friends. On this three-day pleasure trip we explore the sights, shop, dine out and take in a Broadway show. In between these activities I speak on the phone with an attorney who is working with me on the tentative purchase of a house on Martha's Vineyard.

As we talk, I unexpectedly feel a gnawing sensation in the pit of my stomach. I sense that the cause of this agitation has nothing to do with the outcome of this real estate transaction.

That night, while I lay asleep in the hotel room, a jarring, interior disturbance abruptly awakens me. Yanked out of sleep, my heart pounds as rapid-fire shock waves convulse my body. I look at the clock. It's one a.m.

Four hours later, when this acute episode subsides, I open my eyes and stare at the ceiling. Collecting my thoughts, I climb out of bed and write a detailed entry in my private journal.

When I return home to the Cape I learn that on this same night, the beloved daughter of longtime friends took her own life.

* * *

Several weeks later, for the first time since handing my spiral notebooks to Chuck some 20 years before, I share my compilation of secreted journal entries with trusted friends, my husband's cousin and her spouse, a former priest. They find my story compelling.

* * *

That fall the librarian at a church in West Hartford helps me find books about Teresa of Ávila. The last book that she pulls off the shelf has an ominous cover. She says, "You probably don't want to read this one, *The Dark Night of the Soul*, but it's about Teresa of Ávila and John of the Cross."

I say, "I'll take it."

Before I leave the librarian asks if I have a spiritual director. When I answer "no," she writes the name of the Pastor of Spiritual Direction at her church on a newsletter from the Spiritual Life Center.

Synchronicity

I read Gerald G. May's *The Dark Night of the Soul: A Psychiatrist Explores the Connection Between Darkness and Spiritual Growth* cover to cover. Intrigued with its message, words that seem to explain me to myself, I pore through the book twice more: …liberation from attachment…growing freedom for love…self knowledge…obscurity…individual stories…

Hopeful that I might find someone to advise me, I reach out to an author and a publisher who are knowledgeable about Teresa of Ávila, but neither respond to my emails.

Throughout the night I sit at my computer and energetically work on the writing project that I began nine months earlier. At five a.m. I crawl into bed and try to quiet my mind. *Who will believe that these stories are true? Who will help me shape these writings into a book?*

* * *

Two months after my visit to the church library, I meet with the spiritual director that the librarian had suggested. At an hour-long meeting I tell her about my inner experiences, my extensive writings, my research on Teresa of Ávila, and my desire to write a book.

After listening, the pastor explains that she is not the right person to help me. She says that her branch of Christianity has not dealt with the saints since the Reformation and that she has no connection with an editor who might advise me about writing a book. She adds that

Synchronicity

sometimes we have to slow down, that there is no urgency to reach a goal or come to a resolution

As I walk out the door she says, "Wait."

On the top page of my stack of papers, the introduction to a book that I've tried to write, she jots down two names. She says that she doesn't know either woman personally – one is a professor at the Andover Newton Theological School near Boston, and the other is an Episcopal priest at Grace Cathedral in San Francisco.

* * *

Two weeks later, when my husband and I arrive in San Francisco where both of our daughters then lived, I send an email to Reverend Dr. Lauren Artress, the honorary cannon at Grace Cathedral, and ask if she might have time to speak with me.

The next day Reverend Artress, who I have come to know as Lauren, responds, "Call me on my cell phone and let's see what we can work out."

On Super Bowl Sunday 2009, Lauren and I walk to a small café in her neighborhood. While sipping a cup of hot tea she asks, "What is it that you want to do and how may I be of help?"

Five minutes into our conversation she exclaims, "You need a book coach. You have to finish this book and get it behind you. I'll send you the name of someone who may be able to help you."

Synchronicity

As we talk about the synchronicity of events in my life with similar circumstances in the life of Teresa of Ávila, she says, "I don't mean to be irreverent, but so what?"

Understanding my desire to help people, she explains that reincarnation may be an opening, a chance to do things differently or to improve upon what has already been done. She advises me to find my passion in a specific area of interest, start small at ground level, get involved with people, and live life.

A renowned authority on the labyrinth, Lauren tells me that she founded Veriditas to connect individuals to walking the labyrinth as "a spiritual practice that quiets the mind, opens the heart, and grounds the body." She says that walking the labyrinth can be a transformative experience. It has helped many people to focus and find their direction on their spiritual path.

As I listen to Lauren I remember that when I was a senior in high school, I saw the word "labyrinth" for the first time in the preface to my high school yearbook, *Echo*.

When I return home the following week, I contact Catharine Clarke, the book coach who Lauren recommended. When I tell her that Catharine is interested in hearing more about my story and helping me to shape a book, Lauren responds, "Good. Now your toe is in the water. Time to swim."

Uncle Mike

One year after I delve full-time into this writing project, a soul journey, my inner strength is tested.

Prior to our son's wedding, I hear a rumor that I wish to exclude the bride's grandmother from the rehearsal dinner. Aware that in the past, false accusations have triggered my bouts with depression, I keep my emotions in check. In response to this fabrication I turn inward. At center, in the sacred space that opens when I close my eyes, unconditional love floods my heart. As I emanate healing energy, it neutralizes negativity, engenders forgiveness, and restores peace and balance in my everyday life.

* * *

In June 2010, three weeks after my Uncle Mike attends the Cape Cod wedding, he celebrates his 90th birthday. Gregarious and spry, he looks younger than his age. A devoted, loving, and generous great uncle to our three children, he calls them "Big Nieces" and "Big Nephew." When I was a child his pet name for me was "Pal."

A lifelong caregiver, my uncle lives in the ranch-style house in our hometown that he and his beloved wife, Helen, now deceased, bought new in 1958. Self-sufficient, he takes pride in his ability to live independently. A former athlete and coach, this enthusiastic and knowledgeable sports fan was inducted into his local Athletic Hall of Fame in 2001.

Uncle Mike

Alice, also widowed, is my uncle's dear friend and dinner companion. She and my Aunt Helen were coworkers at Hallmark Cards, a distribution center in our hometown, for more than 25 years. Classmates since kindergarten, Alice and my Uncle Mike attended their seventieth high school class reunion together. A memento of this occasion, a bottle of champagne labeled with my uncle's graduation picture from 1939, sits on a shelf in my kitchen.

More than four decades ago, Alice's daughter was one of the friends who walked home from school with me on the last day of eighth grade, the day that I met Chuck, my lifelong confidant.

By the fall of 2010 my Uncle Mike's host of medical problems and physical ailments has caught up with him. He had been diagnosed with non-Hodgkins lymphoma 16 years prior, and soon after he had cardiac bypass surgery and received an implanted pacemaker. Afflicted with diabetes, he suffers from neuropathy. In addition, he has asthma, arthritis, hypertension, edema, and osteoporosis. On a regimen of 12 prescriptions that he takes at varying times throughout the day, he sometimes mixes up his pills. In spite of these setbacks he insists upon living alone, in his own home, taking care of himself.

Now that walking has become more difficult, my uncle uses a wheelchair when I drive him to his frequent doctor appointments. For him, these office visits are social events.

Uncle Mike

Hard of hearing, he chats with his physicians while I listen to their medical findings and take copious notes.

By December my aging uncle is barely mobile. He has fallen twice. In the past two months he's lost 25 pounds. At a follow-up appointment with a geriatric oncologist, the doctor simplifies the diagnosis: the cancer is active and the disease has weakened his bones.

After this office visit I take my uncle directly to a scheduled meeting with a geriatric social worker at the hospital cancer center. She sets his mind at ease by asking him questions about his service in the United States Navy during World War II, his family life, his past jobs, and his involvement in sports. She then talks to him about managing everyday tasks, such as hygiene and meal preparation, and tending to his complex medical needs. She explains that it's no longer safe for him to live at home alone. Finally, she suggests that he consider hiring a home healthcare provider, or, alternatively, that he begins to consider moving into a nursing home or an assisted living facility.

Three days before Christmas, when I arrive at my Uncle Mike's house, I find him in the kitchen, slumped in a chair, resting his head on the round, wooden table. Unshaven, he's wearing dirty pajamas and a torn bathrobe.

Whimpering, he tells me that he has severe pain in his hips and back and that his legs are so stiff and numb that he cannot move. He goes on to tell me that he wanted to back his car down the driveway to get the mail, but that he wasn't able to go down the step from the kitchen to the back porch to get to the garage.

* * *

Initially a difficult adjustment for him, my uncle tells Alice that the quality of his life has improved since he moved into an assisted living facility across the river from our hometown. His clean, spacious apartment is furnished with his favorite belongings. He watches the Sports Channel on cable television. He eats regular meals and raves about the food. He enjoys the recreational activities, the social events, and the company of many longtime friends, including Alice's sister, who are also residents.

* * *

One morning, four months after my uncle moves into assisted living, the staff notices that he is not at breakfast. The nurse checks in on him and finds him resting in bed, congested and feverish.

When I arrive at his apartment and ask how he's feeling, my uncle says, "Paula, I don't know why they're making such a fuss. I just have a cold."

Minutes later, two paramedics and a police officer put him on a stretcher, load him into an ambulance, and take him to the hospital. In the Emergency Room, one of the nurses tells me that my uncle may have pneumonia.

When the diagnosis is confirmed, he is admitted to the hospital. Over the next two weeks his condition deteriorates. The doctors tell me that the antibiotics they are using have not

Uncle Mike

been effective against the pneumonia or the infection, and that the medication may be causing his delirium.

At first they say that his impaired mental status is temporary and reversible, but when his kidneys fail, they report that his condition is terminal.

In hospice care, my uncle cannot eat or swallow. His speech is unintelligible. He does not respond when the doctors ask him to open his eyes, move his fingers, or wiggle his toes. They are surprised to learn that at times, when we are alone, he momentarily escapes from his delirium and speaks to me.

I want to sit up.
I'm hungry. Why can't I eat?
Rub my back.
Can I get up?
Paula, what is happening to me?

* * *

On the morning of May 11, 2011, at my uncle's bedside, I pick up the hospital phone and call Alice, his dear companion. I hold the receiver to my uncle's ear. Although he does not speak, I notice his facial movements – his lips, his eyebrows, his eyelids, his final response to Alice's kind, familiar voice.

In the midst of my uncle's passing I think about my father. In a flash I remember that when he died more than 30 years ago, I felt guilty for having kept my mother and sister's secret from him about the baby that my sister had abandoned, the granddaughter that he never met. I also remember my uncle's false accusation, some 40 years ago, that I had caused my mother's unhappiness.

As this flicker of time intersects with my moment of grief at my Uncle Mike's passing, I realize that the family secret no longer holds any power over me.

Holding my uncle's lifeless hand in mine, my heart opens, the old wounds healing, as I feel enormous love, gratitude, and respect for the man who once called me "Pal."

* * *

In the weeks that follow I return to work on my writing project, for me, a pathway of self-discovery that leads to wholeness and truth.

One night, as I sleep, I inwardly hear an earsplitting explosion, like a gunshot. Inside a black void, an invisible womb, I imagine that my body shatters and disintegrates into fragments.

At that moment my physical body convulses and reflexively lifts off the bed. As I come to consciousness, I'm not sure if I'm dead or alive.

Awakened, I feel that something old inside of me has died to make room for something new. Deep in thought, I recall writing in a previous vignette, "Home from the Seminar," that *"one day I will emerge from the darkness of my metaphoric womb, awaken to my fertility and give birth to my true Self."*

In the process of becoming, as I follow the path of my inner labyrinth – a journey into my deepest self, to center, and back out again – I'm reminded that in life, every ending is a new beginning.

The Labyrinth

In a dream I listen as two men, partners in life, talk about marriage, equality, and justice. The firm pressure of a guiding hand on my upper back awakens me with these inward but resounding words: *Love is boundless…soul has no gender…divine love does not discriminate.*

* * *

In July 2012, the town of Chatham, Massachusetts, celebrates its 300th anniversary. The tercentennial theme is "Find your way here." Spearheaded by local clergy, a labyrinth is gifted to the town. The Reverend Dr. Lauren Artress serves as guest speaker at its dedication.

On the day before the opening ceremony, Lauren, who I met in San Francisco in 2009, facilitates an educational labyrinth workshop at St. Christopher's Episcopal Church. I attend this event with a friend from West Hartford, Connecticut, a landscape architect and labyrinth designer, who I met through Veriditas.

At this workshop, entitled "The Wisdom of the Labyrinth," I reconnect with Reverend Marie David. She and her husband, Reverend James "Jim" David, are co-pastors of St. Mary of Magdala Church, an ecumenical Catholic community located in the chapel at Evensong Retreat Center in Harwich Port. I had met Marie two years prior when a friend and I attended Mass and walked the outdoor labyrinth that graces the grounds there. Along

The Labyrinth

with their parishioners, Marie and Jim exemplify the assurance: "All are welcome here."

During a slide show presentation at the workshop, Lauren explains the history of the labyrinth as an ancient archetypal pattern and its revival as a powerful tool for transforming the human spirit. She shares that, over time, walking the labyrinth as a spiritual practice may deepen our compassion, increase our patience, lesson our judgments, and help us to find our purpose in life that we may share it with the world. She emphasizes that the labyrinth can be used in both sacred and secular settings, and that there is no right or wrong way to walk a labyrinth.

Lauren tells us that when she first began her work with the labyrinth, she used Teresa of Ávila's threefold path to God as a model to describe the process that unfolds during a labyrinth walk: Purgation, Illumination, and Union. As I listen to Lauren's words my thoughts spiral back to a journal entry written 24 years before: "We are all on the same spiritual path. One day I hope to discover a universal language that might help all people to find their way."

I sense that the labyrinth may be this "universal language."

When our group boards a bus to nearby Chase Park where the newly installed Chatham Labyrinth is located, Lauren suggests that we walk the circuitous path of the labyrinth in four stages: Remember, Release, Receive, and Return.

Before entering the labyrinth I take a moment to silently express my gratitude and appreciation for all of life. When I

The Labyrinth

step into the labyrinth I let go of all thoughts, put one foot in front of the other, and open to my unique experience.

* * *

Two months after I attend the Celebration and Dedication of the Chatham Labyrinth, a friend on the Cape invites me to her home to watch a documentary film, "Pink Smoke over the Vatican." A former employee of the diocese of Boston, this friend first introduced me to Reverend Marie David. Her son-in-law, a concert pianist and our landscaper, leveled the ground, planted the shrubs, and helped me to select the stones for the garden labyrinth that graces the front yard of our home on Shoestring Bay.

A longtime friend, a stonemason, installed the three-circuit labyrinth that I had designed on paper. His wife is my friend, Tara, a children's book author.

One week after watching the documentary film, "Pink Smoke over the Vatican," I hear on the news that a professor at Harvard Divinity School reported that the ancient words written in the Coptic language on a scrap of papyrus from the 4th century translate as, "Jesus said to them, my wife." Online I read that the fragment also includes a dialogue between disciples about Mary's worthiness. In translation Jesus replies: "she can be my disciple."

The Harvard professor states that this find possibly references Mary Magdalen but does not historically substantiate that Jesus had a wife. The author of the

The Labyrinth

translated text nonetheless refers to Jesus as a married man though this does not warrant proof.

"Pink Smoke over the Vatican" focuses on the question of ordaining women as Roman Catholic priests. In the film a Roman Catholic priest, Father Roy Bourgeois, shows his support for women called to ordained priesthood. This reminds me of an article I read online, an overview of several books about Teresa of Ávila, in which the reviewer states – in reference to Gillian T. W. Ahlgren's book, *Teresa of Ávila and the Politics of Sanctity* – that Teresa's "idea of sanctity, that one did not have to be a man to be a religious leader, had enormous popular appeal even though she was questioned numerous times by the Inquisition."

Two weeks later, on October 4, 2012, the Vatican dismisses Roy Bourgeois from his order, the Maryknoll Fathers and Brothers, and excommunicates him from the Roman Catholic Church after 45 years of service, 39 as a priest. In February 2013, four months after this dismissal, Pope Benedict XVI announces his retirement from the papacy. He is the first pope to step down from this office in 700 years. Pope Francis succeeded him.

* * *

In her book, *Walking a Spiritual Path: Rediscovering the Labyrinth*, Reverend Dr. Lauren Artress writes, "Jeff Saward, a researcher and author of *Labyrinths & Mazes: A Complete Guide to Magical Paths of the World*, educates us that labyrinth revivals occur when cultures are redefining themselves." She believes

The Labyrinth

that the labyrinth experience can provide a bridge among people of all ages, all races, and all religious traditions.

On October 15, 2014, the annual Feast Day of Saint Teresa of Ávila, Vatican Radio announced a message from Pope Francis: 2015 marks the Jubilee Year for the 500th anniversary of the birth of Teresa of Ávila. A Discalced Carmelite and Doctor of the Church, she was born on March 28, 1515 and died on October 4, 1582.

According to this announcement, Saint Teresa "teaches us that the path to God is the path towards love for one another." Describing her as "a woman of immense spirituality," the Pope focuses on four gifts that Teresa possessed: "joy, prayer, fellowship and being in touch with the realities of her own time." Pope Francis adds that through her writings, Saint Teresa has "perennial relevance" and has given "new impetus and courage for action."

The yearlong, worldwide quincentennial celebration of Teresa's birth began on October 15, 2014 and will continue through October 15, 2015. This milestone in the history of humankind may serve as a universal opening, a catalyst to inspire personal transformation and global change.

* * *

The timing of the culmination of this writing project, my life's work, coincides with the recent arrival of our first grandchild. Beyond the personal elation, for me, the birth of our granddaughter symbolizes an endless continuum of unconditional love.

The Labyrinth

This new life deepens my responsibility to honor and protect the continuum of life by celebrating the feminine legacy passed to me from previous generations, a heritage to bequeath to my children and to their children for generations to come.

In the labyrinth of life, where every ending is a new beginning, I envision this eternal feminine regeneration, and my part in it, as a walk toward center, into the depths of the inner self, the womb of creativity and intuitive awareness, to that sacred space where love unites us all.

* * *

In 2014, on my first trip to Italy with my husband and our dear friends, we drive through the town of Praiano on the Amalfi Coast. As we pass the Church of San Gennaro, I say that my deceased father's name in Italian is Gennaro.

First-generation American, my father was the first-born son in a family who immigrated to the United States from Naples, Italy. When our tour guide, Paolo, tells us that this day, September 19, is the Feast of San Gennaro, the patron saint of Naples, I think of the evergreen bush that my father once grew from a little red berry, aware that the healing power of the living labyrinth resides in all of us and unites us all as One.

Epilogue

In January 2010, on family vacation to celebrate my husband's sixtieth birthday, I find a book, *Half the Sky: Turning Oppression into Opportunity for Women Worldwide*, waiting for me on the bedroom bureau in the island home that we are renting.

Three months before, while watching a television interview on *Oprah*, I listened to the authors, Nicholas D. Kristof and Sheryl WuDunn, reporters for *The New York Times*, discuss the global crises – horrific acts of violence, persecution, and exploitation – that primarily impact women and children around the world. In their book, the authors, husband and wife, present their extensive research and offer viable approaches to combat these atrocities.

* * *

Guidance often attempts to reach us in seemingly ordinary ways, to awaken our consciousness and open our hearts to all of humanity.

* * *

Guided Footsteps is the essence of my life's journey, my walk into the labyrinth, to center and back out into the world. Many people, including all those referenced herein, have enriched my life and helped me find the courage to tell my story. In voicing my truth, I affirm that each person's story is an important one; each person's story makes a difference.

Epilogue

May mine touch you, inspire and encourage you, to embark on your own spiritual journey, to share your own Truth, and to meet your destiny.

* * *

...to *ask* is to raise awareness, to be conscious of the need to nurture and protect the seed of inner knowing...

...to *be receptive* is to be patient and open, to hear the call to love and honor the willingness to serve...

...to *know* is not a function of the mind, but a fullness of the heart...

* * *

In the labyrinth of life every ending is a new beginning, an opening into a new question, an opening of the heart.

* * *

For more information...

If you wish to support **Veriditas**, simply go to veriditas.org and click on the amazon.com logo when you shop online. A portion of your Amazon purchase will be donated to Veriditas.

To find information about **Roman Catholic Womenpriests** in your area, visit romancatholicwomenpriests.org.

To order **Guided Footsteps**, turn to your online retailer such as Amazon or Barnes & Noble. If you are interested in a large quantity order, contact the publisher:

Soul Garden Press
P. O. Box 49
Malden-on-Hudson, New York 12453
soulgardenpress.com
clarke.catharine@gmail.com